MAKING FICTION FUNNY!

HOW TO CREATE STORY HUMOR

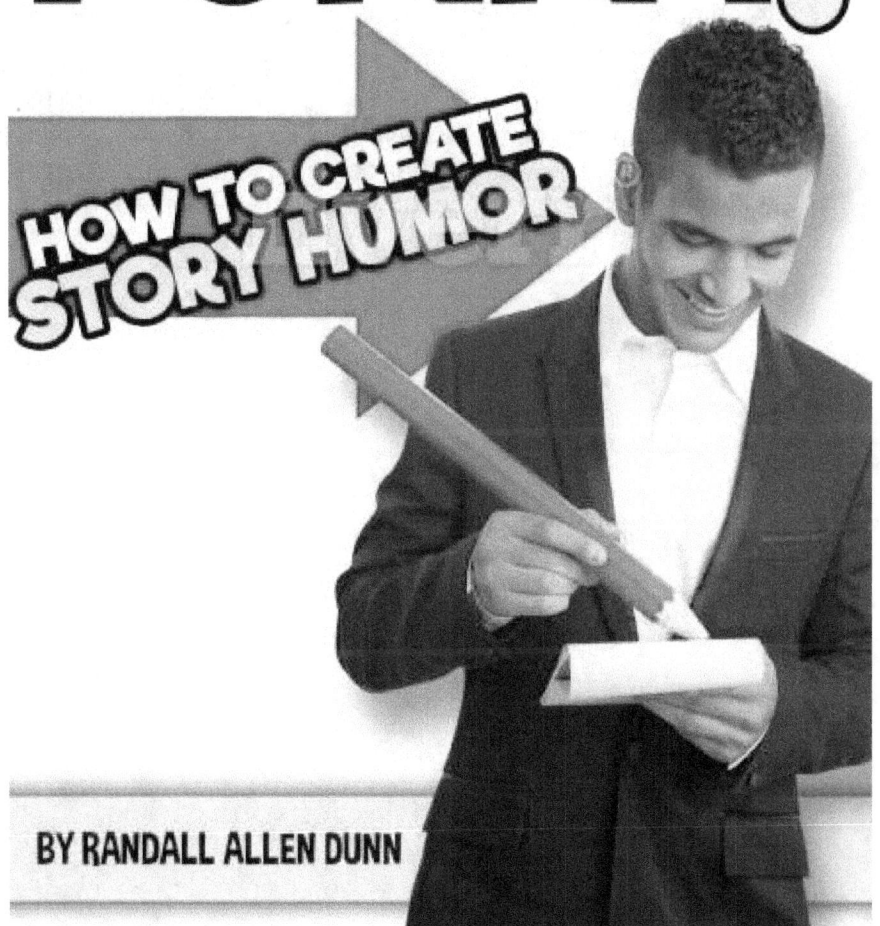

BY RANDALL ALLEN DUNN

Randall Allen Dunn writes stories of action, adventure, and infinite possibility, as well as instructional books about writing.

You can find Randall Allen Dunn at www.RandallAllenDunn.com and follow him on Facebook, Twitter, Pinterest, Goodreads and YouTube.

FICTION

High Adventure: The Solomon Ring of Kilimanjaro

The Red Rider

Den

NON-FICTION

Making Fiction Funny! How To Create Story Humor

MAKING
FICTION
FUNNY!
How To Create
Story Humor

(with Fun Film Examples from
Tommy Boy,
The Princess Bride,
Office Space,
Airplane!
and more!)

by
Randall Allen Dunn

Table of Contents

9

10

So What Are We Doing?

Humor is Good

Welcome to the world of funny!

All right, that's a bit overstated. One thing that should be made clear right away is that the purpose of this book is to help you add humor to your writing. (If you read the title, you may already know this.) Which means exactly that: adding humor. If you are writing a romance, espionage thriller or science fiction story that has no humor whatsoever, and the instruction in this book helps you to add one joke, then my job is done. 0 jokes + 1 joke = 1 joke. Humor has been added.

Hopefully, we will add much more than that. But don't set too high an expectation for your personal writing. This book will not turn you into a stand-up comedian or turn your thought-provoking drama into a hilarious sitcom. We are adding humor to what you already write. We are not transforming your story into a comedy or transforming you into a comedy writer.

So what's the point? Why add humor if it's not a comedy?

Because people need to laugh. We'll explain how that works later. But you know that if a story is funny – even a little bit – you are more likely to enjoy it. Which means people are more likely to buy it, agents are more likely to pitch it, and publishers are more likely to publish it. If you can add humor, you'll make yourself stand out among a vast crowd of bestselling authors who struggle to do anything funny in their stories.

So am I guaranteeing that your book will sell once you learn how to add humor?

Uh ... no. But it will be more enjoyable to read, and should therefore appeal to more people. You'll also have more fun writing it and sharing it with others. The more fun it is, the more likely it is that people will buy it and read it. I can't guarantee your book will sell, but humor will give you a definite edge over your competition.

Consider how humor has helped the success of various series, such as *NCIS, Monk, Buffy, the Vampire Slayer, Psych, Anne of Green Gables,* and the *Harry Potter* books and films. These are not comedies, but they are well-known and loved for their humor. But even series that are not filled with comedy would be far less enjoyable without the humor they add, such as the films of *Star Wars, Star Trek* and *James Bond.*

So now that we have determined humor is good, let's get started.

How This Works

Here are the first things you need to know about this instructional book.

These are working formulas. Things that you can combine together in your story to create humorous scenarios and characters. After you observe a few examples, you will be able to apply the techniques to your own writing with relative ease. With practice, it can even become second nature for you to create something funny.

If this seems too simplistic or mechanical to you – "Take a dry scene, change two details and just add water for instant humor!" – all I can tell you is that it works. The same way that writing works, for those who understand the simple habits and mechanical rhythms of putting a story together. There is a method and technique for writing, just as there is a method and technique for building a bridge, composing a symphony, or designing curriculum for a class. The same is true for writing something funny. When you know how to put the right pieces together, it's easy. Again, we're not turning you into a stand-up comic, but someone who can create enough story humor to entertain and charm your readers.

How This Still Works: Why Movies?

This book uses storytelling examples from popular films, for several reasons. First, movies are more familiar to most people, making them easier to use and discuss as examples. If you're not already familiar with a movie example, it is quick and easy to find and view various film clips online, from a library, or through a rental store. For some people, it can be quicker to watch an entire film than to wade through unfamiliar story examples and try to understand the context.

Finally, while movies are often criticized for being too formulaic and predictable (and therefore assumed to be badly written), this is usually not the case, any more than it is true for literature. In fact, as a visual medium, films must adhere to classic storytelling techniques, such as showing a story's action instead of telling information. Movie stories must be structured in such a way that they work properly, just like well-crafted fiction that endures the test of time. Therefore, most of us can better experience and remember these film examples and later apply them to our writing.

You do not need to watch the film examples, but I encourage you to do so. If you choose not to watch them, you can read the summary of the clip, which will be provided at that point in the book. However, watching the actual movie clips will make it much easier to remember the examples when you write later. Besides, what could be more fun than grabbing some popcorn, loading a movie and telling the people around you, "Everybody quiet! I'm *studying!*"

The first page of each new section will include a list of the film examples you will need for the lesson.

In order to prepare for all lessons, you will need to have access to scenes from the following films, some of which will be used more than once (these are marked with an asterisk *): I am listing the DVD titles here, but you should also be able to find most of the scenes by searching online.

15

Raiders of the Lost Ark

The Princess Bride

Office Space

Pink Panther 2

*Tommy Boy

The Blues Brothers

Ghostbusters

Are We There Yet?

Hitch

The Essential Bugs Bunny: "Rabbit Fire"

M*A*S*H, Season 1: "Dear Dad"

What About Bob?

My Cousin Vinny

Planes, Trains and Automobiles

Christmas with the Kranks

Sesame Street Singing with the Stars: "Celebrity Lullaby"

*North Avenue Irregulars

*The Sure Thing

Airplane!

Cheaper by the Dozen

*While You Were Sleeping

Frasier, Season 6: "A Valentine for Niles"

Tell Me When to Laugh

What Makes It Funny?

MOVIE CLIPS NEEDED:

Raiders of the Lost Ark

The Princess Bride

Office Space

So what makes something funny?

Pick up the average bestselling book – one that's not a comedy – and you'll discover that most writers don't know. Even the funny writers can rarely figure out how you can be funny yourself. Humor is considered to be an elusive and mysterious element that no one knows how to create, but which might magically appear in your story someday, and you simply need to recognize it when you see it.

Baloney.

Some people still view writing this way. As something that just "happens" to writers when their muse descends on them with a burst of inspiration. While this can happen, this is not the normal expectation of productive writers. They work at writing as a job, day in and day out, just like any other job. If their muse shows up with inspiration, great. If the muse is late, the writer should already be writing.

Humor is no different. At least, when it comes to creating humorous characters and situations to make your story more entertaining.

As I researched the topic of writing humor, I found that almost no one could figure out or explain what makes something funny, let alone how to create it yourself.

Fortunately for you, I figured out know what makes something funny. Even better for you, I'm going to tell you.

So let's get started.

MOVIE EXAMPLE: RAIDERS OF THE LOST ARK

We'll begin with a classic example of movie comedy. Watch the scene from *Raiders of the Lost Ark* in which archaeologist hero Indiana Jones searches for Marion in a crowded bazaar in Cairo. Start at the point when he begins shouting her name as he climbs onto a wagon and scans the area, just before he is confronted by a sword-wielding assassin in the middle of the street. After you see Indiana Jones deal with the situation, return here to keep reading. (Note: For this and all movie examples, a summary of the scene is provided on the next page, if you are not able to watch the scene. However, please watch the scenes yourself whenever possible, to get the most out of this instruction.)

SUMMARY: RAIDERS OF THE LOST ARK

Indiana Jones searches for his girlfriend, Marion, who disappeared while he was fighting off a band of local assassins. As he calls for her, the crowd of spectators parts to reveal another assassin, this one grinning as he wields a heavy scimitar. The assassin laughs as he demonstrates his fighting skill, twirling the sword about in an impressive display. Indiana Jones stares at him, preparing for a hand-to-hand fight involving the assassin's deadly sword and his own bullwhip. With a look of exhaustion and irritation, Indiana reaches instead for his holstered gun and shoots the dangerous assassin in the face, ending the fight as he turns away to plan his next move.

How is That Funny?

Was that funny or what?

Note that this movie is, of course, NOT a comedy. But this brief insertion of humor brings extra life and longevity to this classic action-adventure film.

But how did they do it? How was *that* funny?

Consider a person trying to tell someone else about this incident. How funny would it be for someone to say, "Wow, you won't believe this. I just saw two guys facing off in the street. One of them had a huge scimitar sword and the other one had a whip. The guy with the scimitar was showing off his skills and then the guy with the whip pulled out a gun and shot him in the face. Isn't that hilarious?"

No, not really, but thanks for sharing. People would wonder if they should call the police. Seeing a person gunned down in the streets is not funny, in and of itself.

So how did they make this otherwise morbid and disturbing incident into something funny for the story?

The next few sections tell you how.

And Now For Something Completely Different:

Contrast

What is Contrast?

Humor is made up of two components: Contrast and Commonality.

Contrast is the primary component. What makes us laugh is the contrast between what we expect and what actually happens. The bigger the contrast, the bigger the laugh.

Remember this. This is the essence of creating humor. It's all about contrast.

MOVIE EXAMPLE: THE PRINCESS BRIDE

Now watch the scene from *The Princess Bride* which starts the wedding of Prince Humperdink and Princess Buttercup (whose names alone start us laughing). Focus on the elaborate cathedral and the priest as the wedding begins. Watch until you see the response of Inigo Montoya's enemy – the "six-fingered man" – after Inigo confronts him in the corridors. Then return here.

SUMMARY: THE PRINCESS BRIDE

We see an elaborate cathedral where a royal wedding is about to take place. Everything is exquisite and beautiful. The priest motions to everyone as he stands before them in his ornamented robes, looking somber as he prepares to initiate the ceremony.

When he opens his mouth, we discover he has an embarrassing speech impediment of baby talk, as he preaches to the gathered crowd about "mawwiage". He continues his annoying talk as the participants appear uncomfortable, trying to remain proper and take the wedding seriously.

Meanwhile, Westley, Fezig and Inigo break into the palace, intent on rescuing Princess Buttercup from the unwanted marriage. In a corridor, they are confronted by guards, led by the six-fingered man who murdered Inigo's father years ago. After disposing of the guards with his superior swordsmanship, Inigo challenges the six-fingered man, saying the words he has prepared to say for years: "Hello. My name is Inigo Montoya. You killed my father. Prepare to die."

The six-fingered man crouches, preparing to do battle with the assassin. Then turns and runs for his life down the hall.

Shocked, Inigo rushes to try to catch him and exact his vengeance.

Humor is a Surprise

Both the priest and the six-fingered man are hilarious. Why? Because no one expected it (unless you've seen these awesome scenes before, but still, you get the idea).

You can see that the film's director knows this intuitively, whether or not he knows the mechanics of it. But his instinct tells him that a slow build-up to that surprising revelation will make the surprise funnier. So we're led to focus on the elaborate cathedral of an incredible fairy tale wedding. Then we slowly zoom in to see the staunch features of a serious and respectable priest ... only to discover he has the world's silliest speech impediment! At this otherwise perfect and serious celebration, the priest leading the ceremony talks like Elmer Fudd! This is a brilliant device, because it not only surprises us but it also creates ongoing humor, as all the wedding party and guests are forced to remain serious while listening to the baby-talking priest.

Another brilliant surprise is with Inigo's enemy. The build-up to this humorous moment was established early in the film, when Inigo explained his heartfelt quest to avenge his father's murder against a six-fingered man. He recites exactly what he will say to his opponent before taking his revenge. So when we hear him say it in the scene above, the tension is thick, and we expect a battle royal between our hero, Inigo, and the evil six-fingered man who murdered his father.

We don't expect the six-fingered man to turn tail and run.

For your readers, humor is a surprise.

The Mirror Image of Fear

In fact, humor produces a mirror effect of a reader's fearful reaction to suspense thrillers or horror stories. When a story inspires fear, it produces a gasping reaction. The feeling of sudden surprise causes us to suck in air. We also close our body inward as a natural defensive maneuver. We tuck our chin to our chest, curl into a fetal position, or draw the blanket tighter around our shoulders. Why? To protect ourselves. When we're thrown into a dangerous situation, real or imaginary, our body reacts by closing in on itself to protect us from harm.

Humor produces the same gasping reaction of sudden surprise, but is followed by completely opposite actions. We release air instead of gathering it in. Instead of gasping in fear or shock, we guffaw. In both frightening and humorous situations, we are surprised − perhaps even stunned − by the events we experienced. In both cases, it is common for the person to explain their reactions by saying, "I wasn't expecting that," or "I can't believe they just did that." Whether you're scared or tickled by the events, the surprise is what causes your body and your lungs to react.

But while fear produces the need for self-protection, causing us to close inward and shrink away from a threat, humor gives us a cathartic release of tension. Our bodies relax and open up. If something is really funny, our arms might spread out as our head and body roll back. We might even close our eyes or roll on the floor. We're free to put ourselves in a completely vulnerable position because the humorous event makes us feel completely comfortable.

This is why situation comedies (sitcoms) are so popular for prime time television. At the end of the day, some people might want to watch a tense thriller, drama or reality show. But almost everyone loves to have a good laugh, to let all the stress of the day and the latest news headlines evaporate.

This is also why you can appeal to more readers – as well as editors and agents – by building some genuine humor into your stories, no matter what type of story you write. But it must be built into the story as a natural part of it. If you try to insert humor into a story instead of letting it develop naturally from the story components you include, you'll usually end up with weak, contrived humor. Which isn't funny.

The *Raiders of the Lost Ark* scene is funny because we expect the standard movie hero fight scene. One guy has a whip and the other one has a sword, so we expect them to fight with these weapons, which are evenly matched. Not because it makes sense, but because it draws out the action scene, which is what all action-adventure writers do. To paraphrase Indiana Jones, "it's all about the mileage."

But instead of employing the standard literary technique that everyone expected –evening the odds and extending the scene – Indiana Jones surprised everyone by shooting his opponent, finishing the fight in two seconds.

End scene.

Begin laughter.

Writing Ideas: Outthink Your Reader

For your writing, this requires you to outthink your reader. Consider what would normally happen – the boy wins the girl, the underdog wins the fight, the family is re-united – then consider a few things that might happen instead, which are completely contrary to the standard story expectation. List out a few options until you find something funny. For example, the boy wins the girl, only to discover she's really demanding and annoying. The underdog loses the fight, but reveals that he placed bets against himself and just won a million bucks. The family is re-united and they huddle together on their front lawn, free of all their troubles, as the oven's gas leak causes their house to blow up.

These are just a few ideas to get you started.

You might not find any of these scenarios funny, and that's okay. Because there's another element you will need to fine-tune your humor: Commonality.

But first, one final note on creating Contrast.

Caution: Do No Harm

Keep in mind that the humorous contrasts you create must be essentially harmless to the characters. Your characters might suffer terrible misfortune and humiliation, but if they also suffer the loss of loved ones … well, that's not funny. It's too sad for anyone to laugh. Such things can happen in a story, of course. Even in a comedy. But those are the elements for creating drama and tragedy, not humor.

So let your characters blow a job interview for their dream job. Let their teenage daughter refuse to be seen in public with them. Let their family and friends call them a moron. They won't enjoy any of these things, but they can obviously survive them and continue on with their life.

But if your character's leg is bitten off by a shark, if their spouse has an affair and leaves them, if they lose their home and are forced to live on the streets – you have now caused serious physical or emotional harm to a character, from which they might not recover. When a character is truly hurt, people don't feel like laughing at them or their circumstances. When The Three Stooges knocked one another about the head, we all knew they weren't really hurt. If they were, we wouldn't laugh at their pain.

So make your characters uncomfortable, but don't actually hurt them if you're going for a laugh. Make them sweat, not bleed.

I Know Exactly What You Mean: Commonality

What is Commonality?

For our uses, the word "commonality" means "shared perspective". For something to be funny, the intended audience must relate to the experience. That is, they must have enough in common with the story situation to "get the joke". What's funny to one audience is not funny to every other one. So know your audience!

MOVIE EXAMPLE: OFFICE SPACE

Now watch the opening scene of the movie, *Office Space*, as Peter Gibbons tries to navigate traffic during his busy work commute. Watch until the scene ends, when he sees the old man with a walker for a second time.

(Note: Immediately following this scene, another driver is singing along to a radio song laced with extreme profanity. If this will offend you or others in the room, please stop the movie immediately after the example scene.)

After you watch it, return here.

SUMMARY: OFFICE SPACE

On a busy commute to work, the interstate is packed with bumper-to-bumper traffic. Peter Gibbons is annoyed at the stop-start routine, and becomes even more irritated as he sees an old man with a walker, passing him on the sidewalk.

When he notices the left lane of traffic is moving quicker, Peter makes plans to get over. He finds an opening and switches lanes, just as the left lane's progress comes to a screeching halt right in front of him. Once more, he is stuck on the road, making no progress at all.

But now, the right lane is moving at a steady clip, so Peter checks over his shoulder and prepares to switch back. Once more, he successfully changes lanes. But just as he is ready to celebrate his victory, the right lane's traffic also grinds to a halt and he must slam on his brakes once more.

Seeing the left lane's traffic speeding up again, Peter is ready to hit something. Then he squints past the long line of cars and is vexed even more as he spots the old man with his walker, all the way down the block.

Shared Experience

The opening scene of *Office Space* is incredibly funny to anyone who has experienced heavy rush hour traffic. It can be equally funny to anyone who has felt the frustration of waiting in a long line or faced with a no-win situation where Murphy's Law takes over their day. Most everyone has felt this way at some point in life, like they're trying to make progress but they're barely moving.

Commonality is another critical element that makes the *Raiders of the Lost Ark* scene so funny. Up until that time, moviegoers had a shared expectation of how all movie heroes would react when confronting an enemy with a sword. In this case, the aspect of commonality is doubled. We commonly expect a movie hero to engage in physical combat that draws out the scene. But we also know that the common person – that is, any one of us – would be practical enough to use our gun instead. When Indiana Jones does the opposite of what we expect movie heroes to do, doing instead what a *normal* person would do, the audience is completely taken by surprise. Resulting in a classic piece of film comedy for a non-comedy film.

Writing Ideas: Commonality

For your writing, consider everyday scenarios that people might face, to create Commonality. Then develop a scene that emphasizes the feelings or experiences that most people would have in such situations.

For example, a shy high school boy prepares to ask a girl out. When he approaches her in the school corridor, she is surrounded by girlfriends, all of whom stare at the boy like he's a strange bug. The boy feels even more awkward and begins stuttering, making no sense as he tries to tell her he wants to ask her something. He finally cops out, saying he wanted to ask if he can borrow a pencil. She gives him one, along with an odd look, and the boy slinks away, humiliated.

Or show a mother, taking great care to prepare a nice meal for her husband and children, setting the table for everyone. But her teenage son says he plans to just grab a burger or maybe a milkshake for dinner at the video arcade, while her teenage daughter plans to sleep over at her girlfriend's place. The mother tells them both she already made plans for a family dinner and insists that is what they're doing, because no one told her of any other plans. She tells them it's very important to her and their father that they spend more time together as a family.

Then her husband arrives home late from the office, insisting he has to skip dinner because he has more work to finish in his den. The mother nearly loses it, telling them all to sit at the table for a nice quiet dinner together. The husband and children sit like prisoners while the mother retrieves dinner from the kitchen. When she returns, she finds them all sitting in their places, but busy with office work, a handheld video game and a phone texting conversation. She gives up, returns to the kitchen, chops up her chicken dinner into four parts and bags them up with vegetables, then sends each one out with a baggie of dinner. As they head in separate directions, she consoles herself that they'll be eating something healthy.

34

Or show parents of small children waiting in a hospital lobby. After they wait for some time and see other people moving ahead of them, they realize they were supposed to grab a ticket and wait for their number to be called. As they go up front to grab a ticket, they discover the last ticket was just taken, so they will have to wait even longer while new tickets are being printed, but they are assured that the printer only takes twenty minutes to warm up.

These are a few examples to get you started. You've probably experienced some frustration this week, perhaps even today, that many people experience on a regular basis. Use this situation, and your inner frustration, to create a funny scene that uses Commonality. The truer it feels to readers, the funnier it will be.

Who Told You That Was Funny?

Funny to Who?

So you find the Indiana Jones scene funny and I find it hilarious, but I guarantee that someone out there will find absolutely no humor in it.

It might be a war veteran, who never thinks it's funny when someone gets shot and killed. It might be an archaeologist, who is disgusted by the way Indiana Jones misrepresents true archaeology and has a secret dartboard at home with Harrison Ford's face on it. It could be the film's screenwriter, who really wanted to see the scripted fight scene play out.

[Some trivia: the film originally meant to do the standard action hero routine, with a long fight between Indiana Jones and the sword-wielding assassin. Unfortunately for Harrison Ford – and fortunately for the audience – he was too ill during the filming to manage another fight scene, so someone decided Indy should just shoot the bad guy and be done with it. George Lucas was reported to be disappointed, having scripted the extensive fight scene that he looked forward to seeing. But the filmmaking team ultimately chose to add comedy into their action movie instead of piling on one more action scene. Wise choice.]

You can't be funny to everyone. Not everyone will have commonality with you.

So before we get much deeper, be aware of the following reasons that some readers might not "get you", and don't be discouraged if they're not laughing. There can be several reasons for it. (Of course, one reason could be that you're just not funny, but we'll work on that more after the next section.)

Here are various reasons people might not laugh at your story's so-called "humor":

37

They're too old.

The slogan of a Chicago hard rock radio station boasts, "If it's too loud, *you're too old!*"

I have often used this phrase with my kids, who are grade school and preschool age. When they tell me some fireworks or action movie explosions are loud, I tell them, "No, you're just too old." They don't get this, but it entertains me.

The generation gap plays into a lot of humor. I discovered this truth when I shared the movie, *Ghostbusters*, with my parents.

They didn't get it.

It took me a while to figure out that the movie's style of humor was targeted to my generation. My parents *couldn't* get it. My generation was used to the absurdities of Bill Murray acting casual while discussing demons inhabiting a woman's refrigerator. Or observing a giant Stay-Puf marshmallow man tromping through the streets of New York with a big smile and saying, "Now *there's* something you don't see every day."

We understood how this type of comedy works, because our generation's sense of humor was shaped by the comedy of *Saturday Night Live* and similar shows. My parents couldn't follow that, because it was as though they were missing a step of instruction to tell them how this nonsense could be funny. In fact, they were missing an entire generation of instruction on how to appreciate the weirdness of *Ghostbusters*.

Consider the newspaper's weekly section of funnies. I dare you to find humor in every single newspaper strip (not counting the action or drama strips). You can't! Why? Because not all of it is funny to you.

In the same way, not all of it is funny to your mom or dad. But I bet they'll laugh at some of the strips you don't "get". Readers who laugh at *For Better or For Worse, Blondie* or *Family*

Circus are far less likely to laugh at *Calvin & Hobbes, The Far Side* or *Dilbert*, and vice versa. These newspaper strips target the humor styles of vastly different generations.

You might also encounter the opposite problem with readers not getting your humor …

They're too young.

My four-year old daughter, Abby, was telling "knock-knock" jokes to her five-year old friend. I found it very educational.

Here's a taste of their conversation, so you can share in this discovery.

"Knock, Knock," said Abby.

"Who's there?" asked her friend.

"Peanut butter."

"Peanut butter who?"

"Peanut butter on a bicycle that's flying a kite!"

Her friend busted up laughing. Not chuckling. Not giggling. Full out, gut-busting laughter.

But Abby wasn't done.

"Knock, Knock."

"Who's there?" her friend asked, already smirking and ready for the next side-splitter.

"Cookie."

"Cookie who?"

"Cookie with apple juice on your head!"

Again, Abby's friend held her sides and guffawed, while Abby kept the knock-knock jokes coming. I should have been charging her friend for it, because Abby was ready to go all afternoon with her new stand-up routine. She could have been a preschool headliner in Vegas.

Of course, to those of us who are a little older ... well, that's not funny. At all. It's funny to watch them crack up over it, but the joke itself holds nothing humorous.

Unless you're their age.

If you watch a funny movie with young children, you'll learn that their sense of humor is completely different than yours. Things that are absurd in their toddler world – such as Mommy pretending to be a baby or Daddy putting a pancake on his head – are an absolute laugh-riot. Which is why the picture of peanut butter on a bicycle flying a kite is hysterical. Even at an early age, the concept of contrast for humor is understood. However, a child has a different perspective on what constitutes a strong contrast than an adult does.

A final reason someone might not get your humor is that they might have a different cultural experience, in one or more ways.

We Don't Do It That Way

Different cultural experiences can make people view your humor as strange, offensive or even disturbing. What's funny to a Christian might not be funny to a Muslim. What's funny to an office worker might not be funny to a construction worker. What's funny to a stay-at-home mom might not be funny to the CEO of an investment company.

People often don't get a joke because it's not part of their personal experience, which shapes their outlook on life.

Different cultural experiences can be broken down briefly into four areas: Time; Place; Situation; and Knowledge. These can also be remembered as When, Where, Why and How something is funny. We'll go through these quickly before moving on to discuss how to create humorous story situations.

Time – When It's Funny

A person's perspective is greatly affected by the time period they live in, or have lived through. An older person who has lived through the Great Depression has a different view of money and savings than a younger person who grew up in more affluent times. A person who fought in World War II has a different view of war than a person who fought in the Vietnam War. A 1960's hippie has a different perspective on sex and drugs than a 1980's yuppie. They share similar experiences, but those experiences have distinct differences because of the times they lived in.

Even more important, if you write a historical fiction story, or a science fiction story set in the future, the time that your characters live in will impact how they view situations, and therefore how they view humor. During World War II, an American citizen might readily laugh at a racial joke against Germans, and vice versa. But the same joke would be considered offensive to later generations. People living through the Watergate scandal that forced President Nixon to resign would be less likely to laugh at jokes about government corruption, something that had become a sore subject.

The time people live in determines their understanding of other people and nations, their attitudes toward work and education, toward marriage and family, toward religion and freedom. These perspectives determine – and limit – what they will consider funny

Place – Where It's Funny

A person's geographic location also determines their sense of humor. Someone who lives in a southern farm community has a completely different outlook than someone who lives in a busy urban district. Consider how two such people – one a "city mouse" and the other a "country mouse" – would view the concepts of spending money, being a good neighbor, marriage and divorce, proper education, or family values. These all play into whether someone will "get" your jokes.

The environment someone lives in also plays a factor. Although they might live in the same town, a person who lives on a college campus will have a different sense of humor than a person who is living at home with their parents and working a full-time job. This is because they are surrounded by people with a different sense of "place" – that is, a different position in life. The college environment of classes, activities and homework is completely different than the environment of living with parents, dealing with a boss, and managing money.

Situation – Why It's Funny

The current cultural climate has a major impact on someone's sense of humor. As we just mentioned, the events of the time affect how people view their government, other nations, the economy, business, family, religion, and other people. So what is funny during wartime might not be funny during times of peace.

But people in a town whose beloved mayor just died of an illness might not want to hear jokes about malpractice, sick people or death. They might not even want to hear political jokes. Not until their emotional wounds have had time to heal.

A college buddy of mine used to tell people, when they would make jokes about certain things such as an asthma attack or a heart condition, "Hey, my dad died of a heart condition so don't joke about it." He then revealed that he was kidding. One time a friend pulled the same joke on him, then revealed, "My dad actually *did* die of a heart condition, though." He had no hard feelings about it, but my buddy stopped using that joke on people. He didn't want to risk saying the wrong thing again, to someone really facing such a tragic situation. What people have experienced can determine whether they feel free to laugh at certain jokes.

In addition, the situation people are in can influence how the joke is told. The cynicism that people feel toward a corrupt government or struggling economy can lead them to tell more pessimistic jokes than they might otherwise. While people who feel more secure about their living conditions might make fewer cynical jokes about their own situation, and laugh instead at those poor souls living in circumstances that they consider far worse.

Knowledge – How It's Funny,

or You Just Don't *Know* It's Funny!

Inside Jokes require readers to know certain information. Without that knowledge, it is impossible for them to get the joke. (They can get the general idea that something is funny, but can't get the actual joke itself.) This type of humor might use references to popular media, references to local or national celebrities, or puns that require knowledge of certain words and phrases or familiar quotes.

Saturday Night Live, political cartoons like *Doonesbury*, and some television shows like *Psych* all make lots of references to current events and popular media to create humor. Inside Jokes are the trickiest to use, especially when writing, since it requires the reader to know specific information. So you, as the writer, must keep the reader's pool of information in mind. Imagine them sitting in a room with you as you tell these Inside Jokes. Will they know enough about your subject to get it?

Now that we know what's not funny – at least, not to everyone at every time – let's look at how to actually create story humor.

Types of Humorous Contrast

When you create a contrasting situation, the humor can develop naturally. This is how a television sitcom – or "situation comedy" – works. They create a scenario with strong contrast, typically with several strong contrasts. Then they put them together and force them to work in the same environment.

Some of the best sitcoms are structured with comedic contrast.

*M*A*S*H* is a show about an army hospital patching up soldiers to return them to the front lines, but the chief surgeons in charge of this serious duty, Hawkeye Pierce and Trapper John MacIntyre, are class clowns who spend most of their energy chasing women and pulling high school pranks.

Frasier is about Dr. Frasier Crane, a radio psychiatrist whose own self-absorption and neurotic fears constantly ruin his personal relationships.

Home Improvement is about Tim Taylor, a chauvinistic TV host/handyman who destroys more than he fixes, and typically discovers he must embrace his softer side to set things right with his family.

You get the idea. The result is comedy that goes on and on, providing virtually endless fuel for hilarious scenarios.

Let's look at the different types of humorous contrast you can use.

Weird People:
Clowns

Contrast of People: Clowns and Straight Men

MOVIE CLIPS NEEDED:

Pink Panther 2

Tommy Boy

The Blues Brothers

Ghostbusters

Are We There Yet?

Since stories center primarily on people, the simplest and most common humorous contrast to use is a Contrast of People. You can create this by placing two extremely different characters together in the same situation or location, which forces them to interact. Since a bigger contrast results in bigger laughs, we typically strive to make these characters polar opposites.

Think of them like *The Odd Couple*, the Neil Simon play that became a popular film and sitcom, about two divorced men who decide to share an apartment. Unfortunately, they have polar opposite personalities and values: Felix Unger is an uptight neat freak and Oscar Madison is a down-to-earth slob.

Because these two are such extreme opposites, it takes little effort for the writers to create comedy between them. All they need to do is have one character do something that will agitate the other. Since Felix is the uptight one who's already a little agitated, Oscar usually instigates the conflict.

So we just need Oscar to unwrap a fast food burger and leave the wrapper on the living room floor while he watches a football game, with Felix sitting beside him on the couch. The tension and humor mount as Felix stares at the litter near his feet,

49

to which Oscar is oblivious. Until Felix finally says, "Are you going to pick that up?"

Since their opposite values go far beyond the issues of keeping a tidy apartment, a funny scene can develop from several other details.

Oscar can say, "I'll pick it up when the game's over."

"That's what you say during every game. Still, there it sits."

"Yeah, 'cause, still, here *I* sit. The game's not over yet."

"That's not the point. Why not pick it up now and save time?"

"Save time for what?"

"I don't know. To watch another moronic sporting event after this one's over."

"The Morons aren't playing tonight."

"Very funny. Well, I suppose I'll have to pick it up if you won't."

"I'm gonna pick it up. When the game's over."

"Do you know how much bacteria can form in the middle of our floor by that time?"

"Please, tell me."

"I don't know, but that's not the point!"

… and on it goes. Since they are polar opposites in every way, Oscar and Felix can argue about their social life or the lack thereof. Their hobbies and interests, along with their disdain for those of the other person. Their sense of right and wrong, and so on. As long as the contrast remains, humor can develop naturally and easily. The Odd Couple can argue about anything. Whether to cheat on taxes, how to prepare for a date, how to diet and exercise, whether to help a neighbor move furniture. In almost every situation, you can hear the debate starting between them about the correct way to handle a problem. You can probably hear it escalating quickly into a full-blown, voices-raised, door-slamming argument. And within that argument, a lot of very funny things can happen. This was the genius of *The Odd Couple*,

50

pitting two ordinary men with polar opposite values in a shared room and forcing them to try to get along. This same approach of opposite personalities and values has created brilliant comedy between Laurel and Hardy, Hawkeye Pierce and Frank Burns (*M*A*S*H*), Archie Bunker and his son-in-law, Michael "Meathead" Stivic (*All in the Family*), Martin Crane and his sons, Frasier and Niles (*Frasier*), Ray Barone and his parents (*Everybody Loves Raymond*), Shawn Spencer and Detective Carlton Lassiter (*Psych*), and endless pairs of opposite characters throughout comedic history.

So as you try to create humor between characters, remember: write The Odd Couple, over and over.

However, to create genuine comedy with a Contrast of People, it is best to go to the absolute extreme. Even beyond the example of *The Odd Couple*. You want to create characters that are so completely opposite that one of them seems unreal, such as Frank Burns, Stanley Laurel or Dr. Frasier Crane. These characters often act so strangely that they seem cartoonish, compared to the people around them. And more often than not, this is what you want to create great comedy.

You want Clowns and Straight Men.

Clowns

We're not talking about Bozo or Ronald McDonald. For our purposes, a Clown is defined as an abnormal character in a normal world. The way this character thinks and acts is completely foreign to everyone around them.

They might be bizarre in their mindset, like television's Mr. Bean; Pee Wee Herman; or male model Derek Zoolander in *Zoolander*.

They might be constant screw-ups like The Three Stooges; Inspector Clouseau from *The Pink Panther* movies; Tommy Callahan in *Tommy Boy*; or Gilligan from *Gilligan's Island*.

They might be out of touch with the people around them, like 1960's-bound superspy Austin Powers; nerdy father George McFly in *Back to the Future;* or television's insecure radio psychologist, Dr. Frasier Crane.

Or they might be filled with phobias like Bob Wiley in *What About Bob?* or TV detective Adrian Monk in *Monk.*

These characters are in direct contrast to the lifestyles and mindsets of the people around them.

MOVIE EXAMPLE: THE PINK PANTHER 2

Let's watch a clear example of a Clown and how his abnormal thoughts and actions create humor. Play the scene from *The Pink Panther* 2 in which Inspector Clouseau (Steve Martin) visits the Vatican with a team of internationally renowned detectives to investigate the theft of the Pope's ring. Notice how Inspector Clouseau's behavior is completely opposite that of the other detectives, and of most human beings. Watch from the moment Clouseau and the others walk down the corridor, to the brief scene afterward when the Chief Inspector says why he doesn't want to take Clouseau off the case.

SUMMARY: THE PINK PANTHER 2

Inspector Clouseau tries to push ahead of the other detectives to be first through the door to greet the Pope. His Italian counterpart greets the Pope with dignity and propriety, making a sacred vow to restore the stolen ring that demonstrates a kinship with the Pope. Inspector Clouseau then takes over the investigation, sitting beside the Pope and asking him where his big pointy hat is. The Pope does not know, so Inspector Clouseau concludes that he is probably sitting on it.

He makes a weak attempt to repair the squashed hat, then begins addressing the Pope as "Mr. Pope" and interrogating him in a harsh manner, suggesting that the Pope might have stolen the ring itself to collect on the insurance money. The Pope explains that the ring is priceless and cannot be insured. Clouseau proposes the Pope might have sold the ring so he could live in a big, fancy house. The Pope directs him to notice the huge room they're in, and explains that he already does.

As Clouseau continues to question the Pope, he learns that he spent the previous evening looking at the moon to admire the Lord's handiwork. He tells the Pope he has deduced that he is a very spiritual person, through his keen powers of observation. He then asks the Pope's permission to re-create the crime, by assuming the Pope's position of the previous evening.

As Clouseau prepares to re-enact the crime scene, the other detectives discover a clue on the floor and secure it. Then they turn and are shocked to see that Inspector Clouseau has dressed himself in the Pope's official robes. Clouseau asks the Pope again about his precise activities, and walks out on the balcony to re-enact the Pope's study of the moon. He waves his arms in the air as he pretends to observe the moon, completely oblivious to the roaring crowd below, who believes he is the actual Pope coming out to bless them. Noting how much time has elapsed, Clouseau taps his watch for the time, which looks to the crowd like he is cutting them short, and he returns inside.

When the Pope tells Clouseau he then went back out a second time, Clouseau returns to the balcony, waving his arms to observe the moon as the crowd cheers. He considers whether the ring could have fallen somewhere below the railing. As he reaches down to look, he loses his balance and falls off the balcony, to hang precariously. A nun faints at the sight as the rest of the crowd gasps.

We then see Chief Inspector Dreyfus, who hates Clouseau and is delighted by the news article about Clouseau's fiasco at the Vatican. Dreyfus is told that Inspector Clouseau has been ordered off the case, but Dreyfus refuses, wanting to wait until Clouseau does something *really* embarrassing.

An Abnormal Person in a Normal World

As we can see, a Clown insists on acting a certain way that everyone else sees as wrong. It might work sometimes, but in general, a Clown is always the weirdo: an abnormal person in a normal world.

However, a Clown does not have to be cartoonish like Inspector Clouseau, whose antics and mishaps are so consistently foolish that they would have to be scripted. A Clown can be someone more credible, who still appears abnormal to everyone else, simply because they have a polar opposite outlook on life.

MOVIE EXAMPLE: TOMMY BOY

Take a look at Tommy Callahan in the opening scenes of *Tommy Boy*. Watch from the beginning of the film, up until the scene when Tommy reacts to getting his final grade and runs off. Notice how Tommy is the kind of person we might actually know in real life, who always seems to run into trouble. Of course, Tommy doesn't realize that he keeps running into trouble because of his abnormal view.

Watch how Tommy tries to get through a typical day, and the problems he encounters as a result of his abnormal approach.

SUMMARY: TOMMY BOY

Little Tommy is playing in his treehouse when his mother calls and reminds him to hurry up or he'll be late again. Tommy, an overweight grade school boy, climbs down and rushes into the house, smashing right into the closed glass door. He recovers and rushes out the door with his books and lunchbox, too late to catch the bus.

He pushes his way through a bush to take a shortcut through a neighbor's yard, not realizing that he has dropped his History textbook in the process. A dog starts chasing him, so Tommy spills out the contents of his lunchbox to distract the pooch as he keeps running. Another classmate, Richard, rides by on his bike and sneers at Tommy for being late again. Tommy nearly catches the bus as it stops at a crossing, but the bus starts off again, leaving poor Tommy coughing in a cloud of smoke.

As the smoke clears, we see Tommy as an adult, still overweight, still running late, and still coughing up black exhaust as he misses another bus.

He hurries across a college campus lawn, still trying to take shortcuts, and we see he is wearing a backpack and shorts that make him look silly. As he runs down a sidewalk, a terrified bystander is unsure how to get out of Tommy's way. He finally curls into a ball and screams as Tommy passes by him.

Tommy then attempts his standard shortcut through a hedge. He then walks around the hedge, dazed from a blow, and sees that he rammed into a wooden fence that two men are erecting on the other side.

He takes off running again, but slows down to appear cool and relaxed as he greets a couple of pretty co-eds passing by. Seeing his building, he rushes for the door, only to find it already locked. He screams to the heavens, shouting for someone to let him in. Defeated, he sits on the stoop as a girl approaches and enters the building through the other double door, which is unlocked. Tommy looks around to make sure no one has seen his mistake, then hurries inside.

In class, the professor hands out final exams. At Tommy's desk, he sees Tommy huffing and puffing from his run, and rolls his eyes. Tommy looks at the first question on his History final, a fill-in-the-blank question that lists three of the original signers of the Declaration of Independence, one of whom is _____ Hancock. Tommy thinks for a moment, unsure. Then he smirks, certain he remembers the answer, and writes "Herbie Hancock". He looks confident of passing, now that he's off to such an excellent start.

Next, we see several college students gathered in a hall, checking their final grades posted on a wall. Tommy makes his way to the front and finds his name, seeing he earned a D+ for the class. He is shocked, then lets out a shout of victory, thrilled that he actually *passed!* He spurts out his enthusiasm to everyone around him, thankful that he's actually going to graduate. He gives one boy a bear hug, then tells him he wishes they had known one another because this embrace feels a little awkward.

He runs off, doing an impressive flip as he heads off to celebrate.

Abnormal Attempts to Function in a Normal World

Tommy Boy Callahan is a perfect example of a normal person – that is, a person who could exist in the real world – but whose impractical mindset makes him a Clown to others. The way a Clown tries to function doesn't work in a normal world. Tommy Boy can barely make it through a typical day and is overjoyed to pass with a D.

However, whether they seem like real people or cartoonish characters, Clowns don't always need overt or exaggerated actions to be funny. Although the exuberant and aggressive behavior of Inspector Clouseau and Tommy Boy helps add to the humor, the initial humor springs from a Clown's abnormal mindset and actions, which run counter to those of a normal person.

MOVIE EXAMPLE: THE BLUES BROTHERS

Watch the scene from *The Blues Brothers* in which Jake and Elwood Blues attempt to escape a pursuing police car by driving through an indoor mall. Start at the moment when they first enter the mall and watch until they finally make their way back out. Notice that they do not believe they are doing or saying anything strange, and their expressions and reactions are not overt or exaggerated. In fact, it is quite the opposite.

(FYI, the Blues Brothers are also driving a used police car, so try not to get confused about who's chasing who.)

When you're done, return here.

SUMMARY: THE BLUES BROTHERS

The Blues Brothers burst through the glass wall of a store that leads into the interior of the mall, knocking piles of store merchandise and shelving everywhere as people leap out of their way. Jake and Elwood remain calm as they drive through the crowd of screaming bystanders, navigating the mall as two police cars race after them, sirens blaring.

As they continue dodging fixed objects and people, Elwood seems impressed, noting to Jake that the mall has a lot of space. Farther on, they take note of a store window, commenting on the new fashions being displayed.

They finally escape the police, leaving one car overturned as they find their way back out onto the street and freedom.

Calm But Still Abnormal

In that scene, we saw two brothers in dark suits and sunglasses, looking deadly serious and dispassionate as they smashed up tons of store merchandise and caused mass panic by racing their used police car through an indoor mall.

Along the way, they made casual remarks as though they were taking a leisurely stroll. "Lots of space in this mall," and so on.

The humor comes from their casual reaction to the dangerous scenario they have created. A normal person would be tense and nervous, wondering if they'll make it out alive, let alone avoid prison. But Jake and Elwood are such odd Clowns that they're perfectly relaxed in the most outrageous predicaments. They're so calm they could almost be Straight Men. But they're not, because their reactions – however calm and collected – are still abnormal. A Straight Man would be screaming during this reckless scene.

Writing Ideas: Serious-Minded Clowns

You can use the example of The Blues Brothers' irrationally calm behavior in your own stories. This develops naturally if you write about a character who is used to dangerous situations and no longer fears them. One example is the hard-nosed John Casey on the television series, *Chuck.* He's used to taking care of international criminals – and everyone else – with a "shoot first, ask questions later" approach. Whenever the innocent geek, Chuck, suggests doing things without violence, Casey often responds by merely narrowing his eyes at Chuck with disapproval and uttering a menacing growl.

Or you might have a character who is serious like a straight man, but takes himself and his opinions so seriously that he becomes a Clown. An example is the side character, Colonel Flagg, who appears in some episodes of *M*A*S*H*. Colonel Flagg is a government agent who threatens everyone who fails to give him their complete cooperation in his secret operations. He often accuses them of treason or sympathizing with the "Commies".

If your story is really serious and you can't find characters that can be Clowns, just amp up the seriousness of one or more characters, taking them a little overboard – like John Casey or Colonel Flagg – and humor will start to develop.

Clown Costumes

One other item to note: I mentioned that the Blues Brothers wear dark suits and sunglasses. These are their Clown costumes.

What? Aren't clowns supposed to wear long shoes, red noses and giant pink hair?

Not anymore, unless you're at an actual circus. These days, such items would more likely describe a Goth teenager on your block.

But why don't these so-called "Clowns", like the Blues Brothers and everyone else, wear the traditional clown costume if they're supposed to be movie clowns?

The answer is simple: such costumes no longer make adults laugh. Humor involves a surprise, the contrast between what you expect to happen and what actually happens. When a Clown wears an obvious costume, you can see his jokes coming. It might still work for kids, but these exaggerated costumes and theatrical make-up are too obvious to get a laugh from adults. They feel they already know that joke, so the Clown can't surprise them as much.

Which is why modern Clowns – like The Blues Brothers, Mr. Bean, and many others – wear a less obvious costume. But it's still a costume that tells us this person is abnormal and will be the focal point of the story's humor. They sometimes even include make-up, as with Pee-Wee Herman's pasty face and pencil-drawn eyebrows; Groucho Marx' greasepaint moustache, eyebrows and glasses; or Jack Sparrow's guyliner from *Pirates of the Caribbean*. It might also include standard props, like Inspector Clouseau's hilariously tiny car, which he somehow has trouble parking in the first *Pink Panther* remake film. Or Jack Sparrow's non-working telescope and other faulty pirate equipment, down to the waterlogged ship he proudly rides to shore as it sinks beneath him.

Writing Ideas: Dress to Unimpress

You can create Clown costumes through various details in your own writing. You might have a Clown with a bow tie he's constantly adjusting, or greasy hair he keeps oiling and smoothing back, thinking it charms the ladies. You might have a woman with outdated bangle bracelets that keep rattling as she walks, while she makes inappropriate advances to every man she meets. You might even have a poor person wearing clothes that don't fit right, while he makes use of every object he can grab and utilize to get through his day. Costumes like these help us recognize and remember the Clowns, and help prepare us to laugh.

(A side note: Characterizations like this might seem cruel, as though we're making fun of someone for being poor or socially unaware. But one of the original film Clowns, Charlie Chaplin, created his poverty-stricken character, "the Little Tramp", who followed this exact pattern during the Great Depression. The Little Tramp's odd mannerisms and struggle with poverty forced him to make use of whatever he could spare or find, which made him sympathetic and endearing to audiences. Although we do, in fact, laugh at the foolishness of Clowns, we also appreciate how they manage to survive and even thrive. Inspector Clouseau solves the case, Tommy Boy saves his father's factory, and Pee Wee Herman retrieves his stolen bike. And since they made us laugh while doing it, we're delighted to see them win.)

Consider the Blues Brothers again. Their deathly serious outfits match their comedic demeanor, as they deliver monotone lines that seem harmless, except that they deliver them in response to the outrageous situations in which such calm expressions are inappropriate. These Clown costumes are exploited well, to the point that one woman asks them both if they're police. "No, Ma'am," Elwood responds in a deadpan *Dragnet* voice. "We're musicians."

They exploit it even further near the end of the film, pointing out how ludicrous their outfits are. As they prepare to escape the police once again, Elwood says, "It's 106 miles to Chicago. We've got a full tank of gas, half a pack of cigarettes, it's dark, and we're wearing sunglasses."

Rather than comment on the obvious stupidity of wearing sunglasses at night, Jake says, "Hit it."

And the Clowns step on the gas, continuing their hilarious escapade.

Now that we've explored Clowns, let's look at the poor souls who have to put up with them: the Straight Men.

Irritated People:
Straight Men

Not Just for Clowns Anymore

We usually think of a Straight Man in comedy as the one standing right next to the Clown, being forced to put up with all of his foolishness. People like Bud Abbott putting up with Lou Costello, Oliver Hardy putting up with Stanley Laurel, the Skipper putting up with Gilligan, and so on.

We also think of a Straight Man as the one who never makes a joke. The Straight Man simply stands there as a foil to the Clown, the only one who can make us laugh.

But a Straight Man does not always need a Clown to create humor, although this is what usually occurs. A Straight Man can also tell plenty of jokes, which may or may not be funny. A Straight Man can be just as funny as a Clown, but he holds an opposite position.

Put simply, while a Clown is an abnormal character in a normal world, a Straight Man is a *normal* person in an *abnormal* world. That world might be the world of a Clown like Gilligan or Lou Costello, or it might be an unusual situation or a frustrating dilemma. The humor comes from the contrast of the Straight Man's normal behavior as he is bombarded by abnormal people, environments, or activities.

The Voice of Reason

Essentially, the Straight Man is the audience, or the voice of reason. What your average reader believes to be true and right is what the Straight Man will also believe. It is the same principle that is used in *Sherlock Holmes* stories by using the character of Dr. Watson. While Sherlock Holmes' thoughts and methods are difficult to fathom, let alone relate to, Dr. Watson thinks and acts more like the average reader. Therefore, he can ask the type of questions the reader might ask, and Holmes will be forced to explain certain details, allowing the reader to understand what is happening.

For comedic situations, think of the Straight Man as Alice in Wonderland. A young innocent girl in a world of madness, which refuses to follow any rules of common logic or manners. As a result, she becomes frustrated by the behavior of the bizarre creatures she meets, debating with them and trying to introduce reason to the situation, before finally giving up and storming off in a huff.

Alice is a Straight Man. And Alice is us. When confronted with an abnormal world, she simply responds to it with normal frustration, anxiety, irritation and cynicism.

MOVIE EXAMPLE: GHOSTBUSTERS

Now let's watch part of the movie my parents couldn't get. Bill Murray plays Peter Venkman, a scientist with the strange job of catching ghosts. Of course, he doesn't take it any more seriously than he takes anything else in life. Peter Venkman is obviously capable of humor, but his humor in most of this film springs from the bizarre situations he encounters, and his Straight Man reactions to them.

68

Watch the scene in which he accompanies Dana Barrett to her apartment to investigate her report of ghosts in her kitchen, up until the point where Dana tells him his remark makes her feel so much better. Note his cynical jokes and reactions to his bizarre ghost-chasing activities and the methods he employs to do it.

When you're done, return here.

SUMMARY: GHOSTBUSTERS

Dana Barrett enters her apartment with Dr. Peter Venkman, who doesn't worry much about her reports of ghosts there, but is investigating it in hopes of dating her. He pushes ahead of her, making a melodramatic statement that if anything happens, he wants it to happen to him first. He notices her piano near the door and starts playing the highest keys, telling Dana that the ghosts hate that sound and he likes to torture them with it. He announces his presence to the ghosts, as though they are there and afraid of him.

He begins spraying something in the air from a device, like an exterminator spraying for bugs. Dana asks what he's doing and he tells her only that it's technical, which leads us to assume he has no idea why or what he is spraying into her apartment. He finds her bedroom, but Dana tells him nothing ever happened there. Venkman says that's a crime, and Dana starts to realize he is making inappropriate advances. Annoyed, she tells him he acts less like a scientist and more like a game show host.

Cut to the quick, Venkman gets back to business, letting Dana direct him to the kitchen, where she claimed some demon spoke to her from a portal inside her refrigerator. Venkman has her stand back as he cautiously opens the fridge. He reacts with horror … then shows disgust at all the junk food she keeps inside.

Dana is frustrated, insisting there was a monster that called to her before from inside. Venkman insists that his equipment shows no readings of any such activity. Dana asks if he's using the equipment properly. He starts to say he is, but then can only say he *thinks* so.

Dana tells him this means either she's crazy or she has a monster living in her refrigerator. Venkman assures her he doesn't think she's crazy. Dana sarcastically thanks him, telling him that makes her feel *so* much better.

70

A Normal Person in an Abnormal World

It's easy for Peter Venkman to crack jokes about his situation, since his situation is ludicrous. This is a common use of the Straight Man, especially in extreme fantasy situations like those seen in *Harry Potter* stories or on television series like *Doctor Who* or *Buffy, the Vampire Slayer.* In each of these stories, a normal person – Harry, the Doctor's companion, or Buffy, respectively – must confront a world that is shockingly abnormal. In such "Alice in Wonderland" scenarios, it's easy for Straight Men to make hilarious jokes about their bizarre environment by using calm sarcasm, as if their weird situation has some semblance of normalcy.

For example, on the pilot episode of *Buffy, the Vampire Slayer,* Buffy confronts an ugly vampire and casually remarks about his demonic face, "You know, that's never gonna heal if you don't stop picking."

Straight Men can also joke about how strange their own life has become, after being exposed to the abnormal world. Especially if they have been exposed to it long enough to adapt to its weird routines, while retaining a normal person's perspective on them.

For example, in the sixth Harry Potter film, *Harry Potter and the Half-Blood Prince,* Harry jokes about how turbulent his life has become in the "wizarding world". His mentor, Albus Dumbledore, whisks him away to an unknown house with no explanation, and states that Harry must be wondering why he has brought him here. Harry responds, "Actually, Professor, after all these years, I just sort of go with it."

If you are writing a fantasy, science fiction or horror story, or a thriller that involves unusual crimes or attacks, your Straight Man character can add humor by treating abnormalities as he would treat a normal situation. In the *James Bond* film, *Moonraker,* Bond's gadget supplier, Q, presents him with a deadly dart gun to

71

conceal on his wrist, which fires with a convenient flick of Bond's hand. Bond says, "Wonderful, Q. You must get them in the stores for Christmas."

A Little Less Abnormal

Obviously, you don't need a bizarre scenario for a Straight Man to function. But keep the "Alice in Wonderland" concept in mind. For a Straight Man, the world they inhabit is abnormal, perhaps even nonsensical and bizarre. Like Alice, they feel as if they are the only sane person in their environment.

Some examples of Straight Men in less extreme situations are Mary Richards of *The Mary Tyler Moore Show,* as a normal woman surrounded by unusual characters. The grumpy, hard-nosed Lou Grant. The snobbish television chef, Sue Ann Nivens. And of course, the egotistical but clueless anchorman, Ted Baxter.

This same comedy set-up – a Straight Man surrounded by abnormal individuals – has been used on other shows such as *The Andy Griffith Show, Happy Days, Taxi, Murphy Brown, WKRP in Cincinnatti, Cheers* and *Everybody Loves Raymond.* It was also employed twice by classic Straight Man Bob Newhart on *The Bob Newhart Show* and later on *Newhart.*

We also see Straight Men in films like *Kindergarten Cop,* in which an undercover cop must manage a class of unruly kindergartners. Or in *City Slickers,* in which a group of city dwellers try to adapt to the lifestyle of a cattle rancher. These characters can all make plenty of jokes in the midst of their situation, but the humor comes from the contrast between their normal approach to life and the abnormal situation they find themselves in.

Note that "normal" in the above examples only refers to the character's perception of what is normal. It might be routine for some characters to deal with a dysfunctional family, a kindergarten class, or a herd of cattle. But if it's completely abnormal for the Straight Man, you can create comedy with it by emphasizing the contrast between the two worlds.

MOVIE EXAMPLE: ARE WE THERE YET?

Now let's view another example of a Straight Man in a more common situation. In the movie, *Are We There Yet?*, Nick Persons has agreed to transport two kids across the country in order to impress their single mom, whom he hopes to date. But although Nick loves beautiful women, he hates kids.

Watch the scene in which Nick finishes taking Kevin for a bathroom stop at a convenience store, and rejoins Lindsey in his car and tries to clean a stain off of his inside roof. Watch until Nick ends up on the roof of his car and gets struck by an ax, then falls inside. As you watch, notice how Nick's status as the Straight Man is clearly identified and emphasized. When you're done, return here.

SUMMARY: ARE WE THERE YET?

Nick returns to his car with Kevin and gives Lindsey a snack. She disapproves of his lame choice, but he says that was all they had. He then tries to clean Kevin's juice spill off of the top of his beloved car's inside roof. The stain only spreads and looks worse as he tries to clean it, which irritates him more while Kevin laughs.

Nick's friend calls and Nick tells Lindsey to put it on the speaker phone. His buddy asks how everything is going with those brats he's watching, reminding him that "if the kids hate you, the mom won't date you." Nick hangs up in a panic, but it is too late. The kids narrow their eyes at him. Then they exchange secret nods.

The kids tell him they already knew about him and their mom and it doesn't bother them. They tell him their mom likes him, too.

Then Kevin starts having a major asthma attack, and Lindsey sends Nick to get his inhaler from the car trunk. As Nick runs to the back, she locks him out of the car.

Nick doesn't find this funny, and orders her to open the door. Instead, the kids start laying into him, angry that he's just using them to get on their mom's good side. Kevin calls him a "nasty, horny sex-man" who probably wants to kiss their mom. Kevin puckers up against the glass, smearing his open mouth over it, to demonstrate.

Nick insists that he was doing their mom a favor, but they won't listen. Instead, Lindsey sits in the driver's seat and begins adjusting the mirror, preparing to drive away.

Nick boldly stands in front of the car and orders Lindsey to turn off the ignition. He tells her to look at him, insisting that he's serious. She narrows her eyes at him and presses the accelerator, screaming at the sudden burst of speed as Nick leaps out of the way.

She begins driving about the convenience store parking lot in circles as Nick chases after her. Kevin opens the sun roof and starts taunting Nick, making faces and jeering at him.

Nick finally manages to launch himself up onto the car's roof as Kevin ducks inside. Nick squeezes into the opening and hangs upside down, his legs sticking out of the sun roof, as he tries to stop the car. A man leaving the store observes their reckless driving and notes that Nick is setting a bad example for those kids.

Kevin and Lindsey try to fight off Nick, choking him as they tug on his gold necklace chains. Lindsey throws the car into reverse, and they ram straight into the store's statue of a lumberjack, causing the lumberjack's ax to slip from its place. Nick's eyes bulge as the ax swings down onto the roof and hits him right between the legs. The customer, seeing all of this, calls this "Southern justice", as Nick groans and falls into the car.

"I'm serious."

Straight Men are serious. They might be capable of joking around, like Billy Crystal's character, Mitch, in *City Slickers*. They might appear laid-back and easygoing like Nick Persons, the kind of guy you expect to see at a neighborhood barbecue or a Superbowl party. But when they are forced to confront an abnormal situation, they become serious.

Deadly serious.

In *City Slickers*, Mitch is sarcastic and hilarious in his joking assessment of his situation. But that's only because he jokes about every situation in his life. He doesn't actually find his predicament funny, being stuck with his friends on a vacation trip at a dude ranch, where he feels completely out of his element. Especially since he's only there to confront a major mid-life crisis that's causing him to spiral toward depression. Nothing funny about that. At least, not from his perspective.

Likewise, in the scene we just saw, Nick Persons is fighting for his life against the terrorizing monsters that are Lindsey and Kevin. They might not bother most adults, but for Nick, these two kids are horrifying little demons who threaten to ruin his life. So he sees nothing funny about their bizarre "cutesy" antics. He makes his feelings very clear as he demands that they unlock his car door. He even stands in front of his car, ready to defy them both, as he says, "Look at me. I'm *serious.*"

The little brats ignore him, continuing their joyride, which super-serious Nick is desperate to stop.

Thus, the comedy. The angrier Nick gets at the abnormal world of the kids, the funnier it becomes.

"Don't You Realize How Serious This Is?"

Another thing about Straight Men. Not only are they serious about their predicament, they want other characters to know it. Just like Nick Persons tells Lindsey to look at his face and literally *tells* her he's serious, Straight Men typically call attention to their struggles. After all, to the Straight Man – the "Alice in Wonderland" protagonist trapped in a world of nonsense – this is a crisis. Since they view their concerns and priorities as "normal", what they view as a crisis should be a crisis to everyone else as well.

So they try to alert others, explaining how terrible the situation is, often sounding silly as they do it. If poor Nick tries to explain to anyone else how these kids are wreaking havoc on his car and his life, they will assume he is an irresponsible babysitter who's "setting a bad example". If Mitch complains about how hard it is to adapt to ranch life, they'll say he just needs to toughen up and get over it.

Another item to note: like Clowns, Straight Men can wear costumes. The overly casual, hip clothes that Nick Persons wears tell us exactly what type of person he is. He sees himself as a young, cool "player" who hasn't quite grown up yet. Obviously not a father figure to a couple of obnoxious kids. His costume adds to the humor.

A more subtle example occurs on the television series, *Frasier*. Frasier's father, Martin Crane, typically wears the same outfit: a plaid shirt, usually red and black, with tan trousers. Why? Because it highlights his personality, as a practical, down-to-earth man with old-fashioned values. This provides a stark contrast to his snooty, image-conscious son, who typically walks around their shared apartment wearing a business suit.

When Straight Men Turn Funny

Another important note about Straight Men: they don't have to remain Straight Men in every situation of your story. *Frasier* is a perfect example of Straight Men becoming Clowns for a brief exchange, then returning to their usual Straight Man role. Martin Crane is typically the Straight Man to his sons' odd habits and opinions. Both Frasier and Niles are so neurotic, obsessive and socially immature that they keep creating complex problems for themselves, while Martin rolls his eyes at their impractical choices.

However, Martin has an excellent prop that frequently transforms him into a Clown, if only for a few seconds. He insisted on bringing his ratty old armchair to Frasier's apartment, refusing to upgrade to anything nicer. This causes Frasier fits, since it looks horrible planted right in the center of Frasier's fine apartment décor.

In one episode, Martin discovers a hole in the fabric of his chair, and Frasier suggests they replace it. Martin assures him there's no need, as he "fixes" the unsightly hole with a thick strip of duct tape.

In this moment, Martin's odd behavior makes him the Clown, while Frasier rolls his eyes at his father's bad taste. Seconds later, Martin returns to his normal Straight Man role and is rolling his eyes at Frasier's odd ideas. So the Straight Man is not necessarily a character; rather, it is the role that a character assumes to create humor in a scene.

Writing Ideas: Get Serious!

To create your own Straight Man, focus on creating two parts of "Alice in Wonderland". For the Straight Man to be funny, you need to make him an "Alice" and plant him in his version of "Wonderland".

If your character is an image-conscious lawyer running for political office, have his drunk and disorderly brother lose his job and come live with him, to behave in the most appalling ways imaginable when the television cameras are on.

If he's a hard-nosed military veteran who prizes personal discipline and respect above all things, throw him into an environment where such things are least likely to occur. Such as being forced to teach a group of unruly high schoolers.

If she's a shy single woman looking for a meaningful long-term relationship, have her partying friend drag her to a male strip club where men keep pestering her for a one-night stand.

If he's a father trying to raise his young children to be mature and sensitive to others, have his kids play endless practical jokes, like hanging a pail over a door to dump flour on him and his three-piece suit.

These are simple examples, but the idea is to create a "serious" Straight Man character and determine what he values most in life. Then create an environment that makes it impossible for him to have those things, upsetting his entire balance of right and wrong behavior. In other words, determine what makes your straight-laced Straight Man an "Alice", and throw him into the corresponding "Wonderland" where nothing makes sense (to him).

Now let's explore another form of humorous contrast, the Contrast of Skills and Abilities. These boil down to what I call David and Goliath scenarios.

Vote for David, He's Sure to Lose!:

David and Goliath Scenarios

Contrast of Skills and Abilities

MOVIE CLIPS NEEDED:

Hitch

The Essential Bugs Bunny: "Rabbit Fire"

M*A*S*H, Season 1: "Dear Dad"

What About Bob?

Tommy Boy

Horribly mismatched opponents look funny, like a "David and Goliath" scenario. When someone sees their opponent is much bigger, stronger or more talented than they are, it creates a funny moment, due to the obvious Contrast of Skills and Abilities. This device is frequently used in television and movies, usually for a brief instant of surprise when someone realizes he is in way over his head.

The Contrast of Skills and Abilities can be used for humor in two different ways. The first type is a David scenario, in which we root for the underdog. We've all seen such scenes, such as when Marty McFly confronts Biff, the bully, in *Back to the Future,* only to discover that Biff is *much* bigger than he realized. Or *Rocky III,* when boxer Rocky Balboa prepares to fight a gigantic wrestler named Thunderlips for a charity event. As Thunderlips enters the auditorium, Rocky asks his trainer, Mickey, "Why are they carrying him?" Mickey smiles and replies, "He's *walking.*"

These routines have been used dozens of times over. They will continue to be used for quick laughs until the end of comedic time.

But David scenarios aren't limited to obstacles of people. Any monumental task can create story humor if it seems nearly impossible for your David character to achieve.

MOVIE EXAMPLE: HITCH

Watch the scene from *Hitch*, in which dating expert Alex "Hitch" Hitchens meets his next client, Albert Brennaman. Consider the monumental task facing Hitch as he studies Albert, a shy, clumsy, overweight accountant who is obviously dating-challenged. Watch until Hitch tells Albert, "Let's go paint that ceiling." Then return here.

SUMMARY: HITCH

In a voice-over, Hitch explains how he has made it a personal goal to help lonesome men learn how to get the attention of their dream girls. He then states that his new client, Albert Brenneman, is the worst case scenario. As he says this, we see Albert in his office, sitting at his desk with his coffee. Stunned by a newspaper headline photo, he drops his mug, which spills coffee onto his lap and the newspaper. Frustrated, he stands up and begins waving the paper up and down to dry it.

Next, we see Albert sitting on the tiered marble steps of an auspicious office building. Hitch watches him from afar, pulling out a picture of Albert from a portfolio. Albert's close-up self-portrait makes him look sad and distorted, like a funhouse mirror image.

Hitch studies the real Albert on the steps, who doesn't look much better. As Albert eats his lunch, he accidentally squirts mustard on himself. He attempts to clean it, and ends up knocking over the rest of his food and stepping on his pop can, causing it to hiss and spurt pop into the air. Hitch shakes his head as Albert finally recovers, embarrassed and angry at himself.

Hitch introduces himself with a friendly handshake. Albert is amazed to see that "the date doctor" really exists and might be able to help him, as he confesses that he's desperate. At least, when it comes to his dream girl.

Hitch sits down to let Albert talk about her, asking if she knows he's interested. Albert is certain she does not. Hitch asks if she knows he's even alive. Albert reveals his single encounter with her, when he pushed past other eager accountants to loan her his pen.

Hitch is aghast to learn that Albert's dream girl is Allegra Cole, a woman who is clearly out of Albert's league. In fact, she's out of everyone's league. Hitch thinks that Allegra's last boyfriend might have owned Sweden.

84

Albert admits the idea is ludicrous, but he's completely in love with Allegra, and feels she has been dating men who treat her poorly. Hitch laughs at the idea, seeming impressed that Albert "swings for the fence". Albert walks away, realizing this was a foolish idea and there's no hope of ever getting a woman like Allegra to notice him. Hitch stops him, willing to consider helping him.

Albert tells Hitch he's miserable, knowing that Allegra is with the wrong person, but he's so in love with her that he wants her to be happy, even if it's not with him. Hitch tells Albert he is completely out of his mind. Albert agrees.

Hitch smiles, telling him that's a good thing. Albert is surprised, and asks Hitch if that means he thinks he can get Allegra to notice him. Hitch asks Albert if he's ever heard of Michelangelo and the Sistine Chapel. He explains that he is going to be Michelangelo and Albert will be his Sistine Chapel. He leads Albert away with a smile, saying, "Let's go paint that ceiling."

David Scenarios: A Monumental Task

Professional matchmaker Hitch has just met his greatest challenge ever. Albert Brennaman's inept, awkward persona is instantly hilarious because it shows how difficult it will be for Hitch to make him attractive to a woman. Yet Albert's such a likeable guy that Hitch wants to help pair him up with his dream girl.

Unfortunately, Albert's dream girl is Allegra Cole, the rich, beautiful dream girl of every other guy with eyes. Albert is dreaming an impossible dream and Hitch must somehow turn it into a reality. This monumental task not only creates humor, but it also makes us root for the underdogs. Since Hitch and Albert dare to attempt something impossible – the Goliath task – we want to see them succeed. We like them and we're pulling for them, so we're already in a good mood about these characters. This helps prepare us to laugh even more at their upcoming antics, as they try to pull off their outlandish scheme.

Writing Ideas: It'll Never Work!

This is how the Contrast of Skills and Abilities works in a David scenario. Whatever foolish and impossible goal someone attempts – confronting an oversized bully, trying to date the most popular girl in school, demanding a promotion from a stingy boss, stealing the proceeds from a policeman's charity ball – the smaller the David character and the bigger the Goliath task, the bigger the laughs. And the more we want our David character to win.

This is the heart of story humor. Again, we're not always trying to achieve side-splitting comedy. We just want to add enough humor into our story for people to enjoy the story and its characters more. A David scenario is a great way to create humor and – far more important – to make the story and characters more fun and appealing. The Contrast of Skills and Abilities – setting a seemingly impossible goal for your characters to strive toward – is what makes many stories appealing, with or without humor. You can make readers laugh a little along the way to seeing them achieve that goal, by pointing out how crazy it is to attempt such a task.

So just as you create a good Straight Man with the two parts of creating an "Alice" and throwing him into a "Wonderland", you need a "David" character and a "Goliath" task for him to achieve. In the examples given above, you can escalate the humor by making your "David" wimpier and your "Goliath" task more daunting.

If confronting an oversized bully, make David more of a coward who's never been in a fistfight, and make the bully someone who everyone fears, and have him exercise constantly to build up his massive biceps even more.

Make the employee who seeks a raise someone who is least likely to get one. His numbers are down, along with his attendance and his attitude. Meanwhile, make his boss a stickler for office decorum and performance, who can't stomach people wasting his time with petty requests.

Make the thief clumsy and inept as he tries to steal the proceeds from a policemen's charity ball, and have him keep running into one police officer after another as he tries to hide from them so he can pull off his caper.

Again, just some ideas to get you started. Whatever your "David" plans to do, make it an impossible "Goliath" task for anyone to pull off. Then make it just plain stupid for someone like your "David" to attempt!

Now let's discuss something entirely different: Goliath scenarios, when we root for the champion.

Vote for Goliath, Because We Love Watching People Get Beat Up!:

Goliath Scenarios

Rooting for the Master

Goliath scenarios occur when we root for the "Master". The genius who outwits his opponent, through wit, sarcasm, pranks or other means.

We see this in the insults and humiliations delivered by comedians like Groucho Marx, Don Rickles, Bill Murray and Chevy Chase. It's also demonstrated by television characters like Hawkeye Pierce from *M*A*S*H* and Shawn Spencer from *Psych*, as they repeatedly humiliate their opponents and somehow still come up smelling like a rose. We laugh at the Contrast of Skills and Abilities because the Goliath is so clever that his opponents seem to have no hope of defeating him.

The classic example of a comedic Master is Bugs Bunny. As a sarcastic and streetwise cartoon character, he not only manages to dupe and humiliate his enemies, but he also bends every law of physics to gain the upper hand.

TELEVISION EXAMPLE: THE ESSENTIAL BUGS BUNNY: "RABBIT FIRE"

Watch the complete "Rabbit Fire" sketch in which Bugs must outwit both Elmer Fudd and Daffy Duck. Then return here.

SUMMARY: THE ESSENTIAL BUGS BUNNY: "RABBIT FIRE"

Elmer Fudd tiptoes through the forest, hunting rabbits. Rabbit feet are seen skipping somewhere ahead of Elmer, but we then discover they are fake rabbit feet worn by Daffy Duck, who makes rabbit tracks that lead Elmer straight to Bugs Bunny's hole. Daffy calls down to tell Bugs he has a visitor, then hides behind a rock. Bugs emerges and comes face-to-face with Elmer's gun.

Rather than panic, Bugs leans casually on Elmer's rifle and begins chewing on his carrot, about to start a conversation. He warns Elmer he could lose his hunting license for trying to hunt rabbits when it is actually *Duck* Hunting Season. Daffy emerges to argue this point, and the two debate which of them Elmer is entitled to shoot. They repeat back and forth that it is "Duck Season" and "Rabbit Season", each directing Elmer's rifle at the other person. In the heat of argument, Bugs switches gears and says it is "Rabbit Season", tricking Daffy into arguing back that it's "Duck Season" and ordering Elmer to fire as the barrel is pointed at himself. This exchange is repeated two more times, with the same results as Bugs outwits Daffy again.

Daffy then discovers a posted sign that reads "Duck Hunting Season". So he disguises himself as Bugs and reminds Elmer it's Duck Hunting Season. Bugs arrives, disguised as Daffy, and asks where he got the idea that it's Duck Hunting Season. Daffy urges Elmer to read the posted sign, not knowing it now reads "Rabbit Hunting Season". Elmer blasts Daffy once again.

Bugs then tries to tempt Elmer by reading recipes from a cookbook called, "1000 Ways to Cook a Duck". Daffy quickly fires back from a similar cookbook for rabbits, and the two of them list off various mouthwatering recipes. Elmer tells them he's a vegetarian and only hunts for sport.

Bugs and Daffy soon return to their heated argument, pulling one posted sign after another from a tree, each of which reads either "Duck Season" or "Rabbit Season". Finally, they uncover a sign that reads "Elmer Season". Elmer grins nervously, then retreats as Bugs and Daffy dress in Elmer-like hunting gear and pursue him with rifles.

A Genius in Any Season

Bugs Bunny wins. Always. Whatever the threat is, whatever the game is, the comedic Master always triumphs over his enemies, whether they're stupid or brilliant. No one can outwit Goliath, the Master, whether it's Duck Season or Rabbit Season.

We find it funny to watch the Master systematically destroy his opponent, even if it sometimes seems cruel. Of course, this requires that we feel little or no sympathy for the victims, and that the victims are not seriously hurt. They might be humiliated or bruised a little, but never killed or maimed beyond repair.

Beyond that, it's somewhat like watching an episode of *Mission: Impossible.* We don't question whether it's right for a team of spies to infiltrate a foreign government's office, steal valuable merchandise and then frame their enemies for the crime. We're just in awe of the skills and genius they use to do it. (And, of course, their enemies are shown to be evil and deadly, so we are made to feel that they deserve what comes to them.)

MOVIE EXAMPLE: M*A*S*H, SEASON 1: "DEAR DAD"

Now watch a scene from *M*A*S*H, Season 1,* in the episode, "Dear Dad", when Frank and Margaret plan for a romantic evening alone, not realizing that their evening has been sabotaged by Hawkeye and Trapper. (On the DVD, this scene is titled, "Some Enchanted Evening".) Watch from the moment Hawkeye begins describing the nurses at the M*A*S*H 4077th, as well as Frank's "secret" relationship with Margaret. Watch until Hawkeye and Trapper say goodnight to each other. Then return here.

93

SUMMARY: M*A*S*H, SEASON 1: "DEAR DAD"

In a narrated letter to his dad, "Hawkeye" Pierce explains that Frank Burns and Margaret "Hot Lips" Houlihan are having what they presume to be a secret affair, but everyone knows about it. As Frank prepares for a romantic rendezvous with Margaret, Hawkeye and Trapper question what he's up to. They exchange sardonic glances with one another as Frank applies cologne and acts as if he's simply going for a walk.

We then see that, earlier that day, Hawkeye and Trapper had snuck into Margaret's tent, where a sign on the door warns visitors to knock before entering. After stealing inside, Hawkeye reaches a fist out to knock on the door, adhering to Margaret's instructions.

When Frank arrives, he and Margaret are ready for a night of passion. But when Frank tries to blow out the candle, it won't go out. He realizes it's a trick candle and that someone is playing a joke on them. Irritated, they determine to ignore it. But when Frank sits on the bed, it collapses, since the legs have been sawn off. Margaret then discovers pudding smeared on her pillow.

Frank stands to his feet and swears he'll get even with the pranksters as he pounds an angry fist at the center pillar, which instantly breaks in half. Frank and Margaret look up in dismay, just before the entire tent roof collapses on them both as they spout angry threats. Nearby, listening to their moaning, Hawkeye and Trapper say goodnight to one another and settle into a satisfied sleep.

The Master at Work

When we watch a Goliath – the Master at work – we're impressed by their comedic skill and quick wit. By their uncanny ability to escape their enemy's traps, designed to ensnare or even kill them. By the way they turn the tables to humiliate their enemies instead. Seeing Bugs Bunny outwit both Elmer Fudd and Daffy Duck, we can't help but admire how he turns the tide of events against his opponents, no matter what they threaten him with. Since we know Bugs' enemies are just cartoons, and since the victims of other live action Masters are never truly hurt, we can laugh at the torment the Masters put them through.

In the case of Hawkeye Pierce, Frank Burns is presented as a cruel, arrogant buffoon, someone for whom we have no sympathy. Even if we did, it's funny to see the creative genius that Hawkeye and Trapper use to ruin Frank's evening with Margaret, piling one prank on top of another, until they literally bring the entire house (tent) down on them.

The humor comes from seeing how obnoxious the prank is for the victim, and watching how frustrated the victim gets. We see similar barbs made by Shawn Spencer to poor Detective Lassiter on *Psych*, and similar pranks made by camp counselor Tripper Harrison on camp director Morty in the film *Meatballs.*

However, just like Straight Men can tell jokes, the Master does not always need confidence or a strong personality. Their Goliath skills might occur with little or no effort on their part.

MOVIE EXAMPLE: WHAT ABOUT BOB?

Watch the scene from *What About Bob?* in which hypochondriac Bob Wiley gets off the bus in a small town and all the other passengers applaud, glad to be free of him. Watch until

95

Bob agrees to Dr. Marvin's arrangements for a meeting between them and the two men part ways. Then return here.

SUMMARY: WHAT ABOUT BOB?

Bob Wiley steps down from a bus, breathing heavily, holding onto a plastic bag which contains water and his goldfish, Gil. The entire busload of passengers applauds at his departure as Bob catches his breath and the bus drives off. Bob stands in the center of the town and begins shouting at the top of his lungs, calling for Dr. Leo Marvin.

Dr. Marvin, a psychiatrist, exits a nearby convenience store with his wife and children, enjoying his private vacation. His wife says she thinks she hears someone calling his name. Dr. Marvin spots Bob, his most recent counseling patient, and is shocked. He hurries the family into the car to avoid being seen by Bob, but it is too late. Bob runs to Dr. Marvin, overjoyed.

Dr. Marvin is less thrilled. Undeterred, Bob looks inside the car, noting that this must be Dr. Marvin's family. He compliments them all, noting that Dr. Marvin's wife looks much prettier – and younger – than her picture in Dr. Marvin's office.

Dr. Marvin pulls Bob aside for a private talk. Seeing Dr. Marvin's stern posture, Bob wonders if he's done something wrong.

Dr. Marvin reminds Bob that he told him he cannot see his patients while on vacation. He explains that Bob committed a serious breach of trust by contacting him, and even more so by appearing here at his vacation spot. Especially after people told Dr. Marvin that Bob committed suicide. Bob admits that he fibbed a little about that, to learn where Dr. Marvin was vacationing.

Dr. Marvin orders Bob to return home and consult the other psychiatrist on call until he returns, as he instructed before. Bob says he's too afraid of the bus ride and will never make it. Dr. Marvin tells him he traveled here, and the return home will be therapeutic.

Bob insists Dr. Marvin is the only one who can really help him. He begs him, whimpering that he's taking the steps Dr. Marvin told him to take, then begins whining, "I need, I need, I need!"

Dr. Marvin finally agrees to meet Bob in one hour at a public café to talk for a few minutes, so long as Bob promises to return home afterward. Bob relaxes a little and agrees.

As Dr. Marvin walks away, Bob calls out to ask if they could possibly meet sooner. Dr. Marvin turns angrily on him, and Bob says it's fine to meet in an hour.

As Dr. Marvin gets back in his car to drive away, his wife notes that she thinks she *does* look younger than that picture in his office.

Not as Harmless as He Seems

The Master, Bob Wiley, has once again outwitted Dr. Marvin and gotten his way. Why? Because Dr. Marvin can no longer bear Bob's whines and clinginess. To get rid of him and return to his vacation, Dr. Marvin concedes to Bob's insistent request for extra counseling.

It doesn't matter how Bob does it. The point is that in the end, Bob gets what he wants. He wins every time, which is what establishes him as the Master – the Goliath. Because even if he's scared to death of everything around him, Bob somehow manages to manipulate it to his advantage, even if he does it by accident.

What's more, if you look closely at Bob Wiley's behavior and the structure of this screwball comedy, you'll notice that he is aptly named. The movie makes a bit more sense if you watch a Bugs Bunny cartoon beforehand, because *What About Bob?* is, in essence, a live action version of a Looney Tunes film.

Bob Wiley is, in fact, very *"wily"* in his schemes to get Dr. Marvin's attention and help. He's not as harmless as he seems. First, he fakes his own death and pretends to be a detective to get information on Dr. Marvin's whereabouts. Then he crashes Dr. Marvin's vacation retreat and tosses sly compliments to Dr. Marvin's wife, getting in good with the family. Before long, he becomes part of their private family vacation, and the roles of sane doctor and crazy patient are turned upside-down. Bob becomes more accepted and admired by everyone he meets, while Dr. Marvin acts crazier and crazier. To the point that – like a cartoonish Looney Tunes villain – Dr. Marvin finally tries to blow Bob sky high with a pack of dynamite! It's absolutely ludicrous. And hysterical.

What's more, the Contrast of Skills and Abilities is made funnier because of the surprise contrast. While Bob Wiley is obviously a neurotic hypochondriac and Dr. Marvin is a well-

99

respected psychiatrist, we soon learn that Dr. Marvin is actually the one being outmatched. Bob's people skills, determination and sense of humor cause him to outwit and outshine Dr. Marvin again and again. Although he starts out as the clear underdog – the David – he is later revealed as the Master – the Goliath – against whom Dr. Marvin cannot stand.

So whether or not a character seems harmless, and whether or not he realizes the impact of his actions, he can completely disrupt the life and even the mental state of others, like poor Dr. Marvin. This is when we root for Goliath over David, however cruel it might be, so long as nobody gets seriously hurt.

Writing Ideas: Watch This!

When you write a Goliath character, everyone knows the character will win in the end. We just don't know how. Just like watching a *Mission: Impossible* episode or a *Rocky* movie, we don't wonder if the heroes will win. We just want to see the beauty and mastery of their technique in doing it.

Your Goliath could be a fifth degree Black Belt, who is being antagonized by a young street thug. In this case, it's funny to see the ignorant thug get pounded and knocked around the alley. It's even funnier if the Black Belt is an elderly woman, and the thief assumes she's an easy mark as he tries to steal her purse.

He could be a wisecracking psychiatrist whose wife just left him, who takes out his frustration by mocking each of his neurotic patients in such a way that they never notice it. For example, "So, Mrs. Jenkins, you feel you're making progress. Well, as long as one of us thinks so, that's good enough for me."

She could be a harried mother of five small children dropping off kids at school. She hands her baby to a teacher while getting another child out of the car, then pulls a mess of gum off the back seat and slaps it into the palm of another child waiting in line. After a quick hug and kiss, she retrieves the baby from the teacher and straps everyone in for their next drop-off at another school. Before driving off, she suggests that the teacher make sure that other kid washes the gum off of his hands.

Goliath humor can be cruel, but it also gives us a sense of cathartic release when we see people like that Black Belt, psychiatrist or busy mom doing the things we have often felt like doing. We laugh when we see how they get away with it, even if we know they're doing it on purpose.

The point is, they're really good at it. We might feel bad for their victims – a little – but we can't help appreciating and laughing at the Goliath's incredible skills.

Wait, Which One's David and Which One's Goliath?

Twisting the Familiar

Now consider how you can use David and Goliath scenarios to even greater advantage. Since the David scenarios and Goliath scenarios are so familiar, how can you put a fresh spin on it?

Fortunately, familiar scenarios such as these make comedy easy. All you have to do is ask yourself what readers normally expect. Then do something different.

Consider the following example.

MOVIE EXAMPLE: TOMMY BOY

Watch another scene from *Tommy Boy*, in which bumbling Tommy is driving snobbish Richard's car, which Tommy has nearly destroyed by his carelessness. Stuck on the road together, feeling the pressure of trying to sell enough products to save their sinking company, Tommy and Richard are both on edge. Watch from the moment the front hood flips up, blocking their view, to the moment they enter a restaurant and Richard calls the waitress over. Note how both Tommy and Richard hurl Goliath-like insults at one another before and during their fight, and consider what you expect to happen next. Then return here.

SUMMARY: TOMMY BOY

Tommy and Richard are cruising down the highway in Richard's car, its roof and driver's side door torn off, as a result of Tommy's carelessness. Suddenly, the front hood flips up against the windshield, blocking their view. Both men scream as Tommy peeks around the hood at an oncoming semi truck. They veer away from deadly traffic, coming to rest on the side of the road, where they work to catch their breath.

Richard looks irritated, and notes that Tommy was the last one to check the oil at the gas station. Tommy defends himself against Richard's insinuation, insisting he used the correct oil, and the type of oil would have nothing to do with this accident. Richard agrees, but then points to the can sitting upside down on top of the engine and notes that it's hard to close the lid properly if you leave the oil can in. Richard tells Tommy he's worthless.

Tommy hangs his head, realizing he blew it again. He tells Richard he's sorry about the damage to his car, but says not to call him worthless. He's doing his best, but he's not the salesman that his father was. Richard scoffs, saying Tommy's dad could have sold anything to anyone, and he taught Richard everything he knew about the auto parts business. He was like a father to Richard, but even though he was Tommy's real father, Tommy never worked to succeed. He says Tommy just let his dad take care of everything for him, figuring that made it okay for him to be a moron.

Tommy has had enough. He gets out of the car, ready to fight. Richard hurls insults at Tommy about his weight, saying, "Mommy, mommy! The rhino's getting too close to the car!" Tommy mocks Richard scrawny body, saying, "Him afraid. Him just a widdle guy."

Richard steps out of the car, ready to duke it out. They keep hurling insults at one another, each one insisting he's going to tear the other one apart. Tommy's not the least bit worried. He leans his chin forward and offers little Richard a free hit.

Richard clouts him good, and Tommy is dumbstruck.

Tommy pretends not to be phased, acting like he barely felt it.

Richard delivers another crippling blow, leaving Tommy dazed, but still trash-talking.

Richard now picks up a wooden two-by-four from the road and whacks Tommy hard across the side of the head. Tommy admits that was a good one, and falls over unconscious.

Richard sees a Prehistoric Forest tourist attraction beside them and decides to step past Tommy to visit it.

Next, we see Tommy and Richard sitting in a chicken restaurant, waiting in silence at their table as a background song plays, singing "I'm sorry." Recovered from their fight and their rage, they now feel awkward, too ashamed to look at one another.

Tommy asks Richard if he has a mark on his face. Richard looks carefully and tells him he sees no marks, and thought he hit him on the shoulder. Tommy says his shoulder feels fine, but his face hurts. He points to both sides of his face and we see a horrible bruise along his left cheek. Tommy points to both sides of his face, saying it doesn't hurt so much on his right, but it hurts a lot along the line of his left, pointing to the exact area of the bruise. Richard smiles and says Tommy looks fine, then calls the waitress over.

David and Goliath Scenarios with a Twist

Nobody saw that coming. Which made it hilarious.

Throughout the film, *Tommy Boy*, we are reminded of the obvious: Tommy is a big, likeable oaf who can't seem to do anything right because he's uneducated and unaware. Richard is educated and aware, but snobbish and mean-spirited. A clear case of David – the uneducated Tommy – versus Goliath – the book-smart Richard.

So when we're presented with a contest that requires physical instead of mental skills, we're ready to see poor Tommy wipe the floor with the skinny nerd, Richard. Tommy is the underdog we're rooting for, and this is his chance. By the end of this fight, Tommy will finally gain some respect.

Richard beats him to a pulp.

The writers took what was familiar and expected – the long-awaited victory of the underdog, and the classic physical confrontation between two mismatched opponents – and turned it on its ear. The result is a stunning and hilarious surprise.

So if your audience knows what's coming – good! That makes it even easier to surprise them.

Writing Ideas: That's Just What They'd Expect Me to Do

We all know when a story joke doesn't work, and why it usually fails. We see the joke coming. Perhaps we've heard the same joke before, in other books or movies. Perhaps the way the characters act seems too unrealistic or inconsistent with their usual behavior, so the situation lacks Commonality and we don't believe it.

Whichever reason it is, we see we're being set up. Since humor comes from the contrast between what we expect and what actually happens, the joke will never work if we expect it.

So figure out what the reader thinks will happen, then do something radically different.

If we see a little guy with big dreams of scoring a touchdown, when he finally gets the football in his hands near the end of the story, what do we expect? He'll run the distance, dodging his enormous opponents and win the game, right? Right.

So do something else.

Tie up the score, give the little guy the ball, let him run most of the way to the end zone.

Then have him slip in the mud and land flat on his back, as gigantic football jocks fly through the air to pile onto him.

Then what? Well, maybe he's small enough and it's muddy enough that those big guys miss him, or he squirts out from beneath their pile like mustard. He can even slide right across the goal line, still holding the ball.

Sometimes it only takes a few more seconds of action and a little more thought to surprise your audience with something fresh. The more you can surprise them, the more you can make them laugh.

107

I Just Don't See It That Way, and Neither Should You!:

Contrast of Perspectives

My Way or the Highway

MOVIE CLIPS NEEDED:

My Cousin Vinny

Planes, Trains and Automobiles

Christmas with the Kranks

Sesame Street Singing with the Stars: "Celebrity Lullaby"

*North Avenue Irregulars

*The Sure Thing

Airplane!

* = will use more than once

Another useful humorous contrast is the Contrast of Perspectives. This occurs when two or more characters view the same situation differently. It's normally used as an innocent misunderstanding between people, perhaps because they have different information, or because they're using unfamiliar language or slang terms. However, it's often funnier when two people simply have different values or opinions on the situation they both face, causing them to react like to The Odd Couple.

MOVIE EXAMPLE: MY COUSIN VINNY

A scene from *My Cousin Vinny* provides a perfect illustration of the Contrast of Perspectives. (Be advised that this scene uses some harsh profanity and also shows a woman in her negligee as she argues with her boyfriend, with whom she is sharing a hotel. If you find any of this too offensive, you can read the summary provided on the next page.)

Watch this scene, in which unlicensed attorney Vinny Gambini prepares for a hunting trip with the prosecuting attorney for his nephew's murder trial. He hopes to use the opportunity to obtain information about his opponent's plans for the case. Start the scene when Vinny begins to tell his girlfriend, Lisa, what he is about to do. Note the extreme difference in their perspectives about his hunting trip. Watch until Lisa expresses her clear feeling about what pants Vinny should wear. Then return here.

SUMMARY: MY COUSIN VINNY

Vinny tells his girlfriend, Lisa, that he is going hunting with Trotter, the prosecuting attorney. He hopes to gain information on Trotter's case, assuming Trotter will let his guard down if they're out hunting together. Lisa is shocked that Vinny is thinking of shooting a "sweet, innocent, harmless, leaf-eating, doe-eyed little deer". Vinny figures he's a "man's man" and could probably do it. And if he "wimps out", Trotter will lose respect for him. "Would you rather have *that?"* he asks.

Lisa storms off to the bathroom, refusing to listen to any more. Vinny calls to her, asking if she thinks his pants look all right for the trip.

Lisa emerges from the bathroom, and tells Vinny to imagine himself as a deer. She tells him to imagine he's prancing through the forest and spots a brook, and puts his little deer-lips down to drink some of the cool water.

Then suddenly, BAM! A bullet rips through his skull and his brains are lying on the ground in little pieces. She then asks him if he would care what kind of pants the jerk who shot him was wearing.

What Difference Does It Make?

With two different perspectives, the humorous contrast can go on forever, until both characters see eye-to-eye. In the previous example, this will never happen. Vinny is not about to change his mind about hunting with Trotter, which he sees as a vital opportunity to help him win his legal case. Lisa is not about to approve of his killing a harmless little deer. She not only confronts Vinny with her *own* perspective, but she also forces him to consider the perspective of the *deer!*

This is one type of Contrast in Perspectives, when the misunderstanding is Innocent.

MOVIE EXAMPLE: PLANES, TRAINS AND AUTOMOBILES

Now watch the scene from *Planes, Trains and Automobiles*, in which Neal is forced to endure a long car trip with Del Griffith, a salesman he met while traveling. Del has been driving Neal crazy with his ongoing screw-ups, further delaying his trip home for Thanksgiving and causing him countless other problems. But they are finally at peace as Neal sleeps and Del takes the wheel for the night.

Watch from the point where Del tries to remove his coat while driving and gets stuck in his sleeves, ultimately causing the car to spin out of control. Watch until they pull over and Del tries to laugh off their situation by saying, "Wow." Then return here.

SUMMARY: PLANES, TRAINS AND AUTOMOBILES

While Neal sleeps, Del drives through the night at a good speed, listening to music. He attempts to take his coat off to get more comfortable. But as he throws one arm back, a loop of his coat sleeve latches onto a knob on the side of his seat. He struggles but can't move it. So he tries to at least pull his arm out of his other sleeve, but its loop catches on a similar knob.

With both arms trapped, Del is racing down the highway with no way to steer. As he barrels up an exit ramp, he yanks both arms free in a desperate effort, freeing himself as the car spins about in circles. They come to a safe stop as Neal wakes up and asks what's happening. Del tells him nothing's happening and he's fine. Neal suggests he take his coat off to get more comfortable.

Del returns to the interstate, not realizing that he is now driving back down the exit ramp to drive on the wrong side of the interstate, headed toward oncoming night traffic.

A couple driving on the opposite side of the interstate notices Del and Neal's car and tries to warn them. The man honks his horn at them, speeding up to get their attention.

Del honks back, irritated. Neal asks what's wrong, and Del says the other guy must want to race him. Neal sees the other driver wants to tell them something, so he rolls down his window. The driver shouts to them that they're going the wrong way.

Neal tells this to Del, who says the man is drunk. After all, how would he know where they're going? Neal agrees with a nod, and politely thanks the other driver for his useless opinion. The other couple keeps trying to warn them, as Del makes faces at them, showing he knows they've been drinking too much.

The couple shouts to Neal that they're going to kill someone. Neal gradually recognizes the danger as he looks down to see the divide between their car and the other couple. He turns to warn Del, but is struck speechless as he sees the headlights of

113

two oncoming semi trucks. Del tries to understand Neal, who speaks in a strangled voice, and looks back at the road just in time to see the trucks racing toward them.

Their car screeches between the trucks, scraping and sparking against their trailers. In the midst of their horror, Neal imagines them both turning to skeletons, and imagines Del as a tormenting demon who delights in his suffering.

Surviving the passage between the trucks, Del hits the brakes, sending the storage carrier flying from their roof. Neal has his fingers planted in the dashboard, and finds he has dug them so deeply that he has to pry them loose. Del quietly drives to the side of the road to get away from any further traffic. An approaching car swerves crazily to avoid Del and Neal's belongings, strewn all over the road.

Del and Neal get out to survey the damage. Seeing the thick, horrid scrapes along the entire side of the car, Del says it's really not as bad as he thought it would be. He's sure a good mechanic can pound it back into shape in no time. Neal is not amused as Del tries to laugh off the situation, saying, "Wow."

Contrast of Perspectives: Innocent

When two characters view a situation differently, simply by nature of their different perspectives, the Contrast of Perspectives is Innocent. That is, they are not trying to miscommunicate or misunderstand one another. It just happened.

This Innocent contrast can happen in any number of ways. One common way, as seen in *Planes, Trains and Automobiles*, is through Information.

Information (or Lack Thereof)

An Innocent Contrast of Perspectives springs from Information when a character mistakenly believes something to be true. This could be because someone lied to that character or simply because he failed to learn the correct information.

In the *Planes, Trains and Automobiles* scene, Neil and Del assume they are traveling on the correct side of the interstate. This makes them assume the people trying to re-direct them are drunk. After all, as Del observes, "How would *they* know where we're going?"

This same contrast of Information persists when Neal sees the trucks they are heading toward but can't spit out a warning to Del. Since he has not seen the trucks, Del makes no effort to slow down or avoid the crash. Again, the contrast is one of Information, when Neal now realizes what the drivers were trying to tell them but Del fails to notice the danger.

Another type of Innocent contrast is one based on Opinion. This is when characters form different conclusions about the same person or situation.

MOVIE EXAMPLE: CHRISTMAS WITH THE KRANKS

In *Christmas with the Kranks*, Luther Krank has come up with a brilliant scheme to "skip Christmas" and use the money normally spent on the holidays to take a cruise with his wife, Nora. She goes along with the idea but becomes stressed by all the neighborhood pressure to celebrate Christmas, anyway. Watch the scene in which Luther agrees to meet Nora for lunch to discuss her concerns, starting at the point when he meets her at the hospital where she is reading children a story. Note the different Opinions they have about their situation. Watch until the lunch scene finishes, then return here.

SUMMARY: CHRISTMAS WITH THE KRANKS

Nora reads *How the Grinch Stole Christmas* to a group of children at the hospital, as her husband, Luther, arrives in a brilliant white blazer and pants. She notices something odd about his appearance as she squints across the room.

Next, they are seated at a restaurant table where she still stares at him with confusion and horror. She tells him his face looks strange. We see Luther, whose eyebrows are arched high, his entire face looking plastic. He explains he got a Botox injection to remove his wrinkles. He says they froze his face, which is only temporary. As he speaks, he attempts to eat his food, which keeps spilling out of his mouth since he can't move his jaw properly. Nora tells him he should get his money back.

Nora pleads with Luther, telling him they can't keep living this way, refusing to celebrate Christmas. They can't go out, because people keep whispering behind their backs. She can't go home because it's too depressing with no tree, lights or music. And she can't talk to Luther because he's entirely consumed with himself.

Luther insists that is not true. Then as she rails against him for creating a dangerous ice patch on their lawn, Luther begins stabbing his face with a fork, amazed that he can't feel a thing. Nora warns Luther that he could have put one of the visiting Christmas carolers in the hospital. Luther asks if that would be a bad thing.

Nora is appalled, but Luther assures her he is kidding, and he knows how hard this has been for her. He tells her to just hold on for another day and they'll be off on their cruise. After that, he promises her everything will be fine, as he takes a drink which immediately dribbles from his lips to his shirt. Nora is uncertain. Luther again tries to comfort her, but half-chokes on his food again and has to spit something across the room.

118

My Opinion's Better Than Yours

The scene between Luther and Nora is hilarious because of their completely opposite conclusions about their predicament. Nora has started to side with their neighbors. She feels that refusing to celebrate Christmas has become dreary, and the local harassment has made it dangerous. Luther, however, insists that everything is perfectly normal and there's nothing to worry about. His strange insistence of normalcy is compounded by the fact that his Botox injection makes him look and act freakish throughout their meal. Near the end of their conversation, they are no longer even listening to one another.

Similarly, in *Planes, Trains and Automobiles*, we saw Neal's unsavory Opinion of Del as they barely avoided a head-on collision with two semi trucks. Neal came to view Del as a tormenting devil leading him down a path of certain destruction. We can assume Del does not see himself this way, so they have a differing Opinion. Neal's low Opinion of Del colors how he perceives all of Del's behavior going forward.

When Del tried to make light of the accident and put a positive spin on it, Neal silently fumed, viewing the whole event as deadly serious. Like The Odd Couple, their Contrast of Perspectives causes them to share the same experience and draw polar opposite conclusions. Their Opinions of life, death, tragedy, loss, and even what should be considered funny, determine their reactions. If Neal could laugh off the deadly event the way Del did, they would both get along better and be less stressed. But it wouldn't be as funny for the audience.

119

Writing Ideas: I Think Your Brilliant Idea is Stupid

You could write a similar scene between a husband and wife, in which one of them is thrilled about a recent purchase while the other considers it a waste of money. Or a teenager discussing the "cool" clothes he or she is wearing to a party, which the parent deems odd or inappropriate. Or two campaign managers planning out a political strategy, with one of them opting to make their candidate appeal to younger voters while the other wants to appeal to older voters.

However you use it, the Contrast of Perspectives based on Opinions can provide ongoing possibilities for humor if your characters' outlook on life is well-developed for the reader.

A final possibility for a Contrast of Perspectives is a contrast of Different Expectations.

TELEVISION EXAMPLE: SESAME STREET SINGING WITH THE STARS: "CELEBRITY LULLABY"

Watch *Sesame Street's* "Celebrity Lullaby" sketch, in which Elmo attempts to get some sleep and is visited by Ricky Gervais, who offers to help. Watch the entire sketch, then return here.

SUMMARY: **SESAME STREET SINGING WITH THE STARS:** **"CELEBRITY LULLABY"**

Innocent little Elmo sits up in bed, unable to sleep. Enter Ricky Gervais, with a smile and a guitar. He tells Elmo it sounds like he needs a Celebrity Lullaby. He smiles at the camera as he explains that this service provides a celebrity to come and sing a person to sleep.

Elmo asks who the celebrity will be. Ricky asks what he means. Elmo hopes it will be Brad Pitt.

Ricky is a little miffed, and explains the celebrity is himself, Ricky Gervais. Elmo asks if "Mister Ricky" is a celebrity. Ricky gets annoyed, insisting that of course he's a celebrity, or the people at Celebrity Lullaby would not have hired him. Elmo tells him it doesn't matter whether Ricky is a celebrity or not, because Elmo just likes hearing lullabies. Ricky is appeased, but tells Elmo to just be aware that he *is* a celebrity.

He tells Elmo to lay his fuzzy head down so he can sing him a song about the letter "N", which he says is a great letter to fall asleep to.

He begins strumming a beautiful ballad about "nummies", "naptime" and so on.

Then he breaks into the chorus, screaming like a heavy metal singer, "NA-NA-NA-NA NA-NA-NA-NA NA-NA-NA-NA NA-NA-NA-NA NA-NA-NA-NA NA-NA-NA-NA-NAAAAAA!!!"

Elmo sits upright in bed with bulging eyes, telling Ricky it's too noisy. But Ricky keeps screeching away until he finishes the blaring chorus.

As he starts the second verse, he returns to the soft, soothing sounds and Elmo lays back down. Then he returns to the chorus, louder than ever as he stands over Elmo and leans into

121

his face, screaming, "NA-NA-NA-NA NA-NA-NA-NA NA-NA-NA-NA NA-NA-NA-NA NA-NA-NA-NA NA-NA-NA-NA-NAAAAAA!!!"

He adds additional "NA-NA's" to finish off the song, leaving Elmo wild-eyed as he pokes his head out of the blankets at the foot of his bed. Finished, Ricky stands and says, "Nighty-night," and walks off.

Elmo says this did not help him sleep at all. Ricky returns to ask Elmo if he would like a Celebrity Glass of Warm Milk. Elmo says Mister Ricky has done enough. Ricky nods with a smile and leaves.

Elmo jerks with a start as he hears Ricky strum his guitar to tune it offstage.

Didn't See That Coming

The contrast of Different Expectations occurs when one character's Expectation differs from that of another character. In this way, the story capitalizes on the surprise element that creates humor. We identify with the character and what they expect to happen. When something completely different happens, it can be hysterical, as in the *Sesame Street* sketch.

It starts out with the Expectations of Ricky Gervais, who assumes that Elmo will be thrilled to have a visit and even a song from him. Naturally, he's shocked and offended to discover that Elmo doesn't even know who he is.

Elmo has a more natural Expectation, which creates more Commonality with the audience. His Expectation is to receive the promise of being sung to sleep. When Ricky Gervais hammers him with loud screeching and strumming, the contrast is so extreme it becomes hilarious, even when they repeat the joke.

Of course, you can use one or more of types of Contrast of Perspectives in the same funny scenario. So let's put this all together: the Contrast of Perspectives based on Information, Opinion and Expectation.

MOVIE EXAMPLE: THE NORTH AVENUE IRREGULARS

Now watch two scenes from *The North Avenue Irregulars*. In this film, a group of church ladies have volunteered to help track the activities of illegal gamblers which can lead to their arrest. Watch from the moment they start using their radios to communicate with one another, led from the church office by the Treasury Department and Reverend Hill. Watch until the point when Claire — code named "Phantom Fox" — smashes her own radio and tells a man she hates that program.

As you watch, note that the humor springs from the Innocent Contrast of Perspectives, primarily of Information (and misinformation) shared between the Treasury Department and the church ladies they're instructing. But note that humor also springs from Opinions, mainly from the treasury agent's Opinion of how well the women are doing their job, and the Expectations of how some characters expect other characters to act. Then return here.

SUMMARY: THE NORTH AVENUE IRREGULARS

Marv Fogelman of the Treasury Department sighs and prepares to start directing the volunteer church ladies, in whom he has little confidence. He speaks into the radio, saying, "Home Plate, calling all units." He receives a mess of garbled responses as all the ladies talk at once. Irritated, Marv reminds them they can only speak one at a time into the radio.

He asks Claire ("Phantom Fox") to report in. Claire confirms she is stationed in her car outside a pool hall. We see her wearing an expensive outfit, holding her pet poodle in the front seat of her Lincoln Continental. Outside, several unsavory characters stand around her car, one unshaven man bending down to smile through the window at her. Claire says she expects to be murdered at any moment. Should that happen, she asks that someone alert the man who does her hair.

An elderly man comes on the radio, arguing that the women will never find the Mob's "bank", where they keep all their illegal money. Marv gets anxious, trying to find out who the unknown man is. Reverend Hill thinks it sounds like Delaney Rafferty, another member of his church. He gets on the radio and tells one of the volunteer women, Mrs. Rafferty ("Blarneystone") that the whole plan is that the Mob will be less suspicious of women following them. Mrs. Rafferty explains that she can't drive, but assures them no one will recognize her husband, Delaney. Delaney snatches away the radio, and we see he is dressed in drag to look like the other volunteers, as he tells his wife not to use his name over the airwaves.

Another lady, Jane ("June Bride"), spots a suspect exiting a store with a paper bag. At Marv's direction, she tries to describe the man and his car. She tries to identify the car by its color, as Avocado. But as she considers it, she is not sure if it might be something else, not quite Kelly Green but not as dark as Forest Green. Jane finally decides to stick with Avocado.

Marv asks where the car is headed. Jane doesn't know because the car left. Marv yells at her to follow it. Jane obeys, annoyed as she tells Marv not to shout.

As she tails the car in her fiance's Rolls Royce, Marv asks which direction the suspect is heading. "Towards that new boutique," she says. Marv mutters, "She's trying to kill me." Checking the street map, his partner, Tom, decides she means East. Jane takes a wide turn and runs up against a parked car. Reverend Hill asks her if she's all right. She's fine, but nearly in tears as she wonders what her fiancé, Howard, will say about the scratch on his car.

Marv calls Vickie ("Kiddie Car"), but can't get her attention as she tries to deal with a station wagon full of screaming kids. Vickie asks Marv if he can help her by telling one kid to give another kid back his Creepy Crawlers. Marv agrees to do so if Vickie will follow the suspect heading her way. Vickie says she is nowhere near there, though it was her designated position. She says she forgot it's her day to pick up the Cobras little league team, and explains how well they've been doing this season.

Marv walks away from the radio, giving up. Tom suggests giving it to "Klunker". Marv asks if they've tried that one yet. He makes a weary call to Cleo ("Klunker"), who responds immediately that she'll follow the suspect as instructed. However, as Cleo tries to start her rusty pick-up truck, with the used car promo painted on its windshield, the engine won't turn over. Cleo gets out of the truck with her infant nephew and puts him in the stroller, preparing to follow the suspect on foot.

A policeman approaches and asks Cleo if she owns the truck. She explains that it belongs to a used car lot where her husband works. The policeman points out the "No Parking" sign where Cleo parked, and tells her to produce her license and registration. She does so, but as the policeman steps away to check it, Cleo spots a man matching the suspect's description, and decides to follow him on foot. She hurries down the sidewalk, urging people out of her way.

As she gets close to the suspect, parked at a stoplight, Cleo contacts Marv through the radio, now hidden inside her stroller. Since she is standing right beside the suspect, she whispers cautiously, but Marv answers loudly, telling Cleo to get the car's license number. Cleo tries to cover by talking into the stroller and telling her baby to go to sleep, but Marv only gets louder and more insistent. Then the policeman comes running down the sidewalk toward her. Cleo barks into the stroller, telling the baby to pipe down immediately and go to sleep or he'll wish he had. A lady witnessing this tells Cleo that's no way to talk to an infant. Cleo tells her to butt out, causing the woman to gasp as Cleo hurries away, pursued by the officer.

The officer hurries alongside Cleo, handing her a ticket to sign as he warns her that he could cite her for evading arrest. He warns her to move her truck in the next few minutes or he'll have it impounded. Cleo says he's got himself a deal. Huffing and puffing, she finally spots the suspect's car and reports back to Marv. When he tells her to follow him, she tells him she can't, because she's "out of gas".

Tom tells Marv to have Phantom Fox pursue the suspect. Claire is all too happy to leave her seedy position, honking her horn to get creepy men off of the hood of her car. She soon finds the suspect car, and decides to make a wide u-turn to pursue it, nearly running a car off the road in the process. The suspect stops at a park and walks to a picnic bench. Claire ducks down, peering over her dashboard to watch him with the bag of illegal gambling money he's carrying. However, the man opens the bag, removes a sandwich and eats it, then throws the paper bag away.

The next day, Vickie stands in the cereal aisle of a grocery store, looking stern as she watches the same suspect across the room. She loads one box of cereal after another into her cart, until one of her children asks why she is buying so much cereal. "What do you know about shopping?" she asks, then tells them to go play and not bother Mommy. The kids leave and Vickie glances about, making sure no one sees her as she speaks into a walkie-talkie. Back at their home base, Marv tells Vickie and the others to stay alert and watch the suspect closely, to see where they lost the trail of the illegal money bag before.

Vickie sees another man enter the store, also carrying a paper bag as he approaches the suspect. Marv suspects this could be where they pass the money bag. The second man sets his bag down in the first man's shopping cart, next to his paper bag. He flips through some magazines, then snatches up the first man's paper bag. Vickie reports that the men switched bags, and Marv tells her to follow him. "Follow him?" she asks. "Which *one?*"

"The one with the bag!" Marv orders.

"They *both* have *bags!*" she shrieks.

Marv tells her to follow "the new one, with the old bag". Vickie describes the man's appearance. Outside the store, Jane spots him, gives a more detailed description, and starts after him in her fiance's Rolls Royce. Marv tells all units to move in. However, he does not realize the women are all pulling out, one after the other, to follow the suspect in a long single-file line. He tells them all to stay with the suspect.

When the suspect starts speeding away, Marv tells the women they've been spotted and need to peel off. Each one pulls away, giving up the chase. Marv frantically asks who's still following the suspect, but each driver reports that they peeled off as instructed. "They *all* peeled off?" Marv explodes.

Claire then discovers the suspect's car is directly behind her. She reports it and Marv tells her to slow down and let the car pass, but the suspect turns down a side street. He tells her to turn around and follow him, but Tom tells Marv she can't, because it's a one-way street.

Marv tells Claire to wait for instructions, because she can't turn around. Claire says she can't back up, either. Then she offers to try it.

Slamming on her brakes in the middle of the crowded three-lane street, Claire starts backing up as cars honk their horns and swerve to avoid a collision. Claire is oblivious to the destruction she's causing as she continues backing past the side street and turns down it. She spots the suspect in an alley as she passes by and tells Marv she'll double back. She makes a wide U-turn in the middle of the street, causing the car behind her to swerve out of her way. Not seeing the chaos, Marv advises Claire to keep pursuing the car but insists that she not get too close.

At that moment, the suspect backs his car out of the alley and Claire rams right into him. She gets out of the car and asks the irritated driver if he's all right.

Then Marv calls on the radio, asking her for an update of her pursuit in the driver's hearing. She politely excuses herself as she reaches into the driver's front seat to grab a tire iron, which she uses to beat the radio until the noise dies. She returns the tire iron with a smile and casually explains that she never could stand that show.

You Said What?

The scenes you just watched demonstrate all the areas of the Contrast of Perspectives: Contrast of Information, Contrast of Opinion and Contrast of Different Expectations.

When treasury agent Marv Fogelman agrees to direct a group of church ladies in tailing an organized crime syndicate, he doesn't expect much. He receives even less.

Since he's used to working with other agents who know how to tail a suspect, he's frustrated at having to explain the basics to these volunteer women, such as how to describe a suspect and the street they're on. When he asks Jane ("June Bride") to tell him which direction she's driving and she tells him "towards that new boutique", he mutters, "She's trying to kill me." He feels they're making no progress at all with this hairbrained scheme.

Similarly, when the entire group starts following a subject in a single file line, Fogelman tells them to stay with him, not realizing that all of his "agents" are tailing the suspect at once. He also assumes that not *everyone* will follow his instructions to peel off. This misunderstood Contrast of Information creates hilarious chaos.

We also see the Contrast of Opinions at work. Fogelman's Opinion of the ladies and the contrasting Opinions of the women add to the humor. Vickie ("Kiddie Car") decides to pick up a kids' baseball team instead of being prepared to tail a suspect, since she views the baseball team as priority. Meanwhile, Claire ("Phantom Fox") worries that she might be murdered while out in the field, so she asks that someone contact her hairstylist.

Finally, the characters' Contrast of Different Expectations creates humor, such as when Vickie's children ask why she's buying so much cereal for no clear reason, or when Claire assumes everyone will adapt to her decision to suddenly back up on a one-way street.

130

Writing Ideas: If I Told You, I Would Have to Kill You

You can create plenty of funny possibilities with similar situations, whenever someone is trying to conduct secret activities. Either as an undercover agent or police officer, a jealous boyfriend spying on his girlfriend, or a suspicious mother trying to secretly check her teenager's text messages. Any character who doesn't want to get caught doing something clandestine is not only a target for exposure, but a target for great humor.

This is clearly demonstrated when Cleo ("Klunker") must pursue the driver on foot while pushing a stroller with her infant nephew inside. She knows she should wait as the police officer issues her a parking ticket, but she must leave the scene, pushing the stroller as she follows her suspect.

When Marv calls her on the radio hidden in her stroller, Cleo pretends she's talking to her baby nephew, to keep from arousing her target's suspicion. She speaks harshly to end Marv's interruptions, successfully hiding her undercover activity from the suspect. But in the process, she makes herself look like an abusive mother and a criminal as she flees from the policeman.

Whenever your character needs to keep their activities secret, making up random explanations for their odd behavior, you have material for great comedy.

Now that we have fully covered the Contrast of Perspectives that is Innocent, let's look at those that are Intentional.

I Meant to Do That!: Sarcasm

Contrast of Perspectives: Intentional

When a character (or a writer, as we'll discuss later) presents a different perspective on purpose, the Contrast of Perspectives is Intentional. That character is deliberately presenting their alternate view of a situation, in order to demonstrate their own cleverness or superiority over other characters.

In other words, they are using Sarcasm.

MOVIE EXAMPLE: THE SURE THING

Watch the scene from *The Sure Thing* in which Walter "Gib" Gibson arrives late to his English class and we are introduced to his English teacher. Watch until she says, "Clean it up, Gibson." Then return here.

SUMMARY: THE SURE THING

The professor tells everyone that this week's assignment is to re-write last week's assignment. As the entire class groans, she says, "Remember, 'as the dog returns to his vomit, so does the fool to his folly.'"

As if on cue, Walter "Gib" Gibson arrives late to class. He apologizes to the professor, saying he's sorry he's late but there was this really big problem ... and he's late because of it. She gives him a less-than-tolerant glare, saying nothing as Gib sits and shrugs to a friend beside him.

The professor hands back individual papers to students, giving them her critiques. She tells one girl that when she told her before to develop her own style, she did not mean to dot her i's with little flowers. She also tells her not to use colored ink, as it strains the eye. Gib notices Alison, a girl beside him, taking copious notes. "You sure take a lot of notes," he whispers. She glares at him.

Bored, Gib takes out an envelope he received from his best friend, Lance, who had pressured Gib to attend college with him on the beaches of California. The postcard contains a picture of a beautiful girl in a swimsuit. Gib flips it over to read Lance's message: *This is the ugliest girl in California.*

Gib looks at the picture again, stunned, as the professor continues returning papers to each student. She sees that Gibson is distracted as she tries to return his paper, and peers down to see the picture he is fixated on. Gib finally comes to attention as she stands over him. "Mister Gibson," she says. "I realize how important voyeurism is to your daily life, but ... do you mind if I take up a few minutes of your time?" He smiles and says, "Sure". "Thank you," she says, bubbling with gratitude.

She tells him she really enjoyed his paper. Gib is surprised. She says she can't remember the last time she saw so much detail on "How to Eat Pizza Without Burning the Roof of Your Mouth". Gib and the class laugh as the professor smiles.

"Unfortunately," she says. "Whatever whimsical qualities your paper evokes are obscured by a morass of marginal grammar, *creative spelling,* and, I believe, sausage stain." Gib laughs and tells her it's actually pepperoni.

She frowns and drops the paper on his desk. "Clean it up, Gibson."

That's Not Really What I Meant

When a character uses sarcasm, they are pretending to believe something which they actually do not. If other characters are insightful enough, they can pick up on the fact that the character is lying. The warehouse workers aren't *really* hoping the work day will stretch out longer. The blind date doesn't *really* think his bow tie makes him look more attractive. And the English professor we just saw doesn't *really* think any of the students' writing is any good.

In the same way, she is using extreme sarcasm when she politely asks Gib to put away his picture of a girl in a swimsuit so that she can "take a few moments of his time" to teach his class. She adds further insult to embarrassment by referring to the "creative spelling" he employs in his paper.

In a later scene of *The Sure Thing*, the professor reads a student's work aloud, saying, "He was a man, that's all. A man like any other man. A man like *no* other man."

She blinks at the girl who wrote it, then hands back her paper, saying it's "very interesting" and tells her she has a "flair for ambiguity." The pleasant lilt in the professor's voice makes it sound like she's complimenting the student. She's not. But one has to see through the sarcasm and the charm to pick up on the joke – the alternate perspective of the professor. By reading between the lines, we can discover what she *really* thinks, and the joke is even funnier because most people are not in on it. It becomes an Inside Joke, funny only to those who can share the professor's perspective and know she is creating an Intentional Contrast of Perspectives.

Characters can also create this contrast without using sarcasm. Their body language and even their lack of response to a person or situation can make their inner feelings clear, even if they don't say a word.

MOVIE EXAMPLE: THE SURE THING

Now watch another scene from *The Sure Thing*, when Gib goes to a bar and, after a brief fantasy about the girl he hopes to meet, finds himself face-to-face with an overweight drunk. Watch from the moment the man asks to sit down beside Gib, until the point when Gib orders him some spritzer. Notice how the waitress acts toward the drunk. Also note how Gib uses verbal sarcasm. Then return here.

SUMMARY: THE SURE THING

While sitting on a barstool, Gib is shaken from his daydreams by an extremely overweight man who asks if he can sit beside him. Gib says yes, and the man says, "Thank you kindly. … kindly." He is drunk and a little wobbly but manages to sit, with folds of flab rolling over his sides. An attractive waitress comes to the bar to give an order to the barkeep. The drunk addresses her, and the waitress turns slowly to give him an impatient glare as she continues chewsing her gum. The drunk tells her he got another sweepstakes ticket in the mail, but he can't decide if it's worth the effort to send it in. He asks her if she thinks he should bother. She ignores him and returns to her duties.

The drunk privately tells Gib that the waitress claims she's from Paris. He refuses to believe that, because Paris women don't give people a hard time like the women do here. He says to a Paris woman, sex is an art.

At the other end of the bar counter, an older man wearing a cowboy hat speaks up, saying he went to Paris with his wife once. Then he says, "Boy, am I glad *she's* dead."

The waitress returns to the bar counter with another order. The overweight drunk talks to her again, causing another roll of her eyes. He tells her he had fried food again today. He says he knows he shouldn't have done it, but he couldn't help himself. He asks her if she thinks he lacks self-discipline. She says nothing, continuing to chew her gum as she walks away.

The drunk asks Gib, "What's wrong with me? I'm a good-looking guy."

This is obviously not true, but Gib says he *is* a good-looking guy, and so is Gib. The man at the far end of the bar says, "We're all *three* good-looking guys." Gib agrees, and says that it's Christmastime, so he's going to buy both men a drink. The man in the cowboy hat asks for a beer. Gib asks the drunk what he wants. "Oh, something light," he says.

138

"Like a Chablis?" Gib asks with some humor in his voice.

The man asks for a Spritzer.

Gib calls the bartender, saying, "Barkeep. Bring this man a trough of Spritzer."

What Do You Really Think?

When the drunk tells the waitress he ate fried food again and asks if she thinks he lacks self-discipline, she could have responded with a cutting remark. But it's much funnier for us if she simply walks away. We know what she's thinking when it's the same thing everyone else would think about this poor overweight drunk. She can roll her eyes, grunt with irritation, or ignore him and go about her business, as she does in the scene. We know she has a low opinion of him – her Intentional Contrast of Perspective – by the way she refuses to even talk to him. His silly questions and banter tell us why.

Meanwhile, Gib is friendly, but obviously shares the waitress' opinions. He uses Sarcasm to entertain himself at the man's expense, asking if he wants a light Chablis and then ordering him a trough of Spritzer. Gib is creating his own inside joke, with himself (and us) as the audience. Why? Because he's funny and clever, and this is how he entertains himself when no one else is there to enjoy his jokes. He's the Goliath – the Master of humor and put-downs. And although it can be cruel, we laugh at his expert technique in jokes and wordplay.

This plays into another form of Intentional Contrast of Perspective, when the contrast comes directly from the author, to be understood by the audience alone. This is Satire.

Surely You Can't Be Serious!: Satire

Two Parts of Satire

In Satire, the joke is made directly to the audience, not to the other characters. The author uses the Intentional Contrast of Perspectives to make the readers feel clever or superior to the other characters, as the author and reader make fun of the story itself.

The humor for Satire springs from two elements: Mimicry (Parody) and Mockery.

Mimicry – or Parody – is the imitation of someone or something, and the humor is based on how accurately it is imitated. The best example of this is when the *Saturday Night Live* comedy crew imitates a president or celebrity. In the 1990's, when they did a sketch involving newly elected president Bill Clinton and his wife, Hillary, the audience roared when Hillary insisted on joining a discussion by stating that she is the "co-president". There was nothing inherently funny in her statement. What made it funny was the accurate reference to the way the real Hillary Clinton described her White House role as "co-president" rather than First Lady.

Mockery is when the story makes fun of a situation, by viewing it from a different perspective. This is usually the perspective of the author, who points out the flaws or foolishness of the original situation.

For example, in *Paul Blart: Mall Cop*, a security guard ends up trapped inside a mall as he tries to stop a band of thieves. This situation mimics the plot of the action movie, *Die Hard,* in which hero John McLane taunts his adversaries with lines like "Yippee-cay-yay". Paul Blart's character mocks this aspect when he launches a scuba diving tank at one thief, after taunting him by saying, "Scuba dooby doo."

Another scene combines both Mimicry and Mockery for the full effect. In a scene of *Die Hard,* John McLane tends to his battle wounds by backing against a wall and sinking to the floor to bandage his bloody shoulder. *Paul Blart: Mall Cop* imitates this scene, as Blart also backs against a wall and sinks to the floor in the same fashion to fix his damaged shoulder, producing excellent Mimicry. But we then see his wound is a mere scrape, to which he applies a "Hello Kitty" Band-Aid, in perfect Mockery of the original scene.

Now watch a complete scene that puts these elements together.

MOVIE EXAMPLE: AIRPLANE!

Watch the scene from *Airplane!* in which Ted recalls his first meeting with Elaine. Watch from the moment Ted begins telling his story to the point when he finishes and the woman beside him hangs herself. Note the various bizarre humorous events within these scenes, which are made obvious to the viewing audience, while the characters seem unaware of them or treat them as normal. Then return here.

SUMMARY: AIRPLANE!

On board a plane, Ted starts to dreamily discuss his first encounter with his lost love, Elaine, to an older woman who obviously does not care. A flashback scene begins, as Ted narrates that he met Elaine in one of the roughest bars ever, where a fight broke out every night. We see a close-up of hands from people playing cards. One person grabs the other one's wrist and finds extra cards hidden beneath their sleeve. The two players begin a savage fight, and we then see they are two young girls in scout uniforms. They continue fighting in a bestial manner until one girl throws the other one into the bar's jukebox, which then begins playing "Stayin' Alive", the disco theme song from the film, *Saturday Night Fever*. Everyone in the bar suddenly begins moving to the center dance floor, performing disco moves.

Ted leans against the bar counter in his white Navy uniform. He spots Elaine across the room and immediately falls in love with her. Stunned, he asks the rough-looking man standing beside him to pinch him to make certain he's not dreaming. The man gives Ted an uncomfortable look, then cautiously moves away.

Ted narrates that fate was on his side that night, and we see a man stab Elaine's dance partner in the back. As the man struggles to remove the knife, Elaine mimics his struggles, assuming he is doing dance moves. The man finally falls over and Ted approaches Elaine. They are entranced with one another at first sight.

Ted removes his navy jacket, revealing a disco dance outfit with a white vest and blue sleeves. He tosses his jacket aside and strikes an impressive disco pose. Then his jacket is tossed back at him by someone offscreen.

Ted and Elaine begin an amazing dance together. Elaine is impressed by Ted's disco moves, which become more and more elaborate. He soon begins squatting and doing an amazing

144

Russian dance, defying gravity as he leans further backward. Someone offscreen starts tossing him balls to juggle.

The scene ends with Ted and Elaine sharing a slow dance, late into the night. Suddenly, the two female scouts crash into the bar, still carrying out their vicious brawl.

We return from this flashback to the present day, where Ted is relating his tale aboard the airplane to the elderly passenger beside him. We see her feet dangling lifelessly beside his head, as he continues talking, oblivious, saying, "I hope I haven't bored you too much."

You Get It, Right?

In Satire, the author is winking at the audience. They're pointing out something funny to the reader, the only person who's in on the joke. The characters within the story are completely unaware.

In the *Airplane!* scene, humor comes from Mimicry of the dance scenes from the film, *Saturday Night Fever,* down to the disco dance moves and signature John Travolta outfit. It also comes from Mockery, making fun of the film's disco maneuvers as Ted performs impossible dance tricks to wow the crowd.

The film also makes Mockery of its own storyline, which is patterned after traditional disaster movie and romance plots. When Ted sees Elaine across a crowded room, he falls in love at first sight. So much so that he asks the stranger beside him to pinch him and make sure he's not dreaming. In movie romances, the lovers often act as if they're the only two people in the world. In a more realistic scenario, when someone asks a stranger to pinch him, the stranger moves away. In the same way, it makes Mockery of the seedy bar, described as a rough place. Then we see it's so rough that even the local girl scouts are in a knockdown brawl.

Writing Ideas: Get it? Get it?

Satire can be tricky to use for narrative writing. Again, it requires that your reader have the correct knowledge to be in on the joke. So it's more important than ever to know your audience.

I heard of a *Star Trek* novel in which an English police phone booth mysteriously appeared on the bridge of the starship Enterprise. A man stepped out of the box, dressed in a long scarf, glanced at the crew and said, "Oops, sorry." Then he stepped back into the police box and it disappeared, after which the regular story resumed.

This is a hilarious moment for people who know the character of *Doctor Who.* For everyone else, it is confusing and pointless. But since most science fiction readers – especially those who read *Star Trek* novels – would be familiar enough with the *Doctor Who* series to get the joke, it was worth inserting. It would hardly be funny if placed in the middle of a Tom Clancy novel.

If your readers are likely to get it, you can add satire to your story by including a United States president whose description matches that of an existing president. The same for any celebrity that your readers would likely recognize from your brief description. (Just be careful not to lampoon your character so much that you run the risk of a lawsuit from the person you're satirizing! Don't make your caricature so insulting that the person wants to come after you.)

In the same way, you can satirize groups or social events. For example, in the *James Bond* film, *Tomorrow Never Dies,* Bond is called in for a mission by his superior's secretary, Miss Moneypenny. Unfortunately, Bond is busy with his latest love conquest. As Moneypenny hangs up, she discovers her boss, "M", standing directly behind her. "Don't ask," Moneypenny says. "M" responds, "Don't tell." A brilliant satirical jab at the "don't ask, don't tell" policy for allowing homosexuals in the military, enacted shortly before the film came out.

Also note that, while it normally provides humor, satire can also be used for valuable symbolism. For example, the television series, *M*A*S*H*, took place during the Korean War, but for viewers it mirrored the existing Vietnam War conflict. This allowed the series to explore controversial topics about Vietnam in a way that felt less abrasive or awkward for viewers.

Writing Ideas: Yes, I'm Mocking You

A simpler use of satire would be to point to elements of your own story, rather than referencing people or events outside of it. For example, in one of my novels, *The Red Rider,* a teenage girl, Helena, tells her four-year old sister, Suzette, they can't play much longer since it's getting late. Suzette grumbles, then assumes their father's stern voice, saying, "'It's almost dark, girls. We don't wanna be caught out after dark.'" Suzette's perfect imitation – Mimicry – is confirmed as Helena stifles a smile. Suzette's Mockery becomes genuinely funny when their father calls them into the house soon afterward, saying, "It's almost dark. We don't want to be caught out after dark."

This story also provides an excellent example of the value of humor, since it is basically an action-adventure horror story. Any and all humor to break up the tension makes such a thriller more fun to read, and appeals to a wider audience.

Now let's look at a final type of humorous contrast: the Contrast of Personal Expectations.

That Wasn't Supposed to Happen:
Contrast of Personal Expectations

The Best-Laid Plans …

MOVIE CLIPS NEEDED:

The Sure Thing

Cheaper by the Dozen

*While You Were Sleeping

Frasier, Season 6: "A Valentine for Niles"

* = will use more than once

     The Contrast of Personal Expectations is the contrast between what a character hopes will happen and the chaos that happens instead. It might not be literal chaos, but it is chaos to the character and their Personal Expectations. For example, if Oscar Madison, the classic slob of *The Odd Couple*, comes home to find that Felix, his neat-freak roommate, has cleaned and organized his messy room, this is actually a good thing. But to Oscar, it's complete chaos.

     As we discussed early on, this contrast is the essence of what creates humor. In this case, however, it is specifically what a character expects to happen (not what the audience expects), often built up with high expectations, and the resulting situation that dashes their hopes, placing them in an awkward or even dangerous situation.

     When this type of chaos mounts and continues, it creates great comedy as the character's situation grows worse and worse.

MOVIE EXAMPLE: THE SURE THING

Watch the scene from *The Sure Thing* when Gib and Allison are stranded after Allison realizes she has lost all of her money. Watch from the moment they are sitting and moping on the side of the road, until the point when Gib says, "Well, maybe one'll come up." Then return here.

SUMMARY: THE SURE THING

Gib and Allison don't get along well, as they hitchhike cross country to reach friends for Christmas vacation. Unfortunately, Allison lost her wallet that contained all of their traveling money, so they are stuck sitting on the side of the road at night, with nowhere to go. They mope in silence.

Alison finds a stick of gum in her coat pocket and takes it out. She notices Gib staring at her, and she stares back at him, irritated. He looks away, feeling awkward. She proceeds again with her gum, but as she is about to put it in her mouth, Gib tells her he's starving. She reluctantly tears the stick in half and gives him one. He thanks her and they begin chewing.

He tells her he's freezing to death, and she glares at him. He looks sheepish. Then he says he just swallowed his gum. She tells him to stop complaining and try to look on the bright side.

It suddenly begins pouring rain, drenching them both. He nods at her, then they jump up to find shelter. He leads her to a nearby shack. They run inside and sit happily on a bench. Then they realize they're still getting rained on. They look up and see the roof is only a lattice.

They flee the shack and head for a nearby trailer, but find it locked. Gib sarcastically notes that this is a good thing. "It's important that this place should have an airtight security system ... in the middle of *nowhere!!!*"

He grabs a rock to beat on the doorknob. Alison looks through her purse for a useful tool and happily discovers a credit card. She tells Gib.

Gib shakes his head. "Credit cards work on a completely different kind of lock," he tells her as he continues beating the doorknob.

"You don't understand," she says. "I have a *credit card.*"

153

Gib slowly grasps her meaning, as he slows his bashing motion. Alison's face falls as she remembers a problem: her father told her specifically to only use the credit card in the case of an emergency.

Drenched to the bone, Gib casually suggests, "Well, maybe one'll come   up."

But There IS No Bright Side!

In *The Sure Thing*, Gib decides to take Allison's advice to look on the bright side instead of complaining. And, of course, that's the moment it starts pouring down rain. Their positive Personal Expectations are immediately crushed by the chaos that ensues.

Typical of a Contrast of Personal Expectations scenario, things are already bad and they quickly get worse. When Gib and Alison try to escape the rain, they find a shelter but discover it has no real roof. Then they find a trailer but discover it is locked, despite Gib's complaint that it's in the middle of nowhere. Gib's final loss of control over the mounting chaos adds to the humor.

The more a character fights to maintain his hopes for what he thought would happen, the funnier the scene becomes.

MOVIE EXAMPLE: CHEAPER BY THE DOZEN

Watch the scene from *Cheaper by the Dozen* in which Tom Baker – the Straight Man played by Steve Martin – tries to manage his household of wild kids while his wife is away. Watch from the moment his eldest daughter arrives at the house in a business suit, to the moment that Tom sits in his closet while his two youngest sons taunt him after he hangs up the phone. Then return here.

SUMMARY: CHEAPER BY THE DOZEN

The outside of the Baker house is literally crawling with kids, one of whom is rappelling down the wall. A snooty neighbor sees the chaos and comments that all the children are going to end up on milk cartons. Nora, the eldest daughter, drives up to the house and steps out, dressed in a smart business suit. She kisses one of her sisters and happily walks inside.

Within, Tom Baker is on the phone talking strategy for the school football team he coaches, while he also tries to make dinner for the family mob. Behind him, kids are playing and running about in every direction.

One child enters and tells Tom their brother threw a dart at their sister, and that she assumes he will be punished. He hurries to set his injured daughter on the counter and pretends to be frightened at the sight of her wound, to make her laugh. His other daughter examines the pasta and tells him "this goo is on fire." Tom pretends he is not burning dinner, insisting he likes it spicy that way. Nora enters and starts to talk but Tom immediately tells her to find him a bandage.

His twelve-year old daughter, Sarah, enters and tells him that no other kids on their block do chores. He tells her they're not like other kids. She sarcastically asks, "So why do we live here?" Irritated, he orders her to unload the dishwasher.

Sarah discovers her brother's jock strap inside the dishwasher. Not wanting to touch it, she grasps it with two fingers but finds it steaming hot and flings it away, to land in the pasta. Tom pulls it out of the pot with tongs and frowns, saying, "Pasta de la *crotch.*"

As he holds up the jock strap covered in sauce, his son enters and sees it, asking if that's blood. Tom smiles and tells him too late that it's not, as his son vomits on the kitchen floor. Tom makes a sour face, then calls, "Cleanup on Aisle Twelve!" His son steps away and another son, Mike, comes rushing to help. He

156

steps in the pile of vomit and slips, falling flat on his back. He stands up, disgusted, and asks his dad if he still needs help cleaning up. Tom says, "No, you've mopped up most of it with your back." Mike looks sick and trudges away.

Nora enters to hand Tom the bandage he needs, telling him her brother, Jake, got a bucket stuck on another child's head. Then she frowns, saying that if her parents ever get home, could he tell them that she just got a new job. She walks out, discouraged, as Tom tries to chase after her.

Then his wife, Kate, calls. He tries to tell her how well he's handling all the kids himself while coaching his football team full-time, as toys fly past his head and one son hangs upside down from a rope outside the window. His youngest twin sons chase after him with toy guns and start firing at him relentlessly.

Tom retreats into a closet to escape the chaos as Kate tells him her book tour is going fine, but she really misses the kids and wants to talk to one of them. He tells her it's a bad time for that, because they've all started a study group for the kind of math the parents don't grasp. His face takes on a plastic, delirious expression as he tells her how wonderful it is that the kids are studying and helping each other.

He ends the call as his youngest sons taunt him from the other side of the door, ordering him to come out and take it like a man. He continues to smile with a stunned expression as a hatchet blade cuts through the wooden door.

It's All Under Control – Really!

In a Contrast of Personal Expectations, the more your character fights to maintain order and preserve his ideal Expectations, the funnier the ensuing chaos becomes. As Tom tries to convince his wife (and himself) that everything is under control, the surrounding chaos proves how wrong he is and how dangerous his predicament is becoming. The widening Contrast of Personal Expectations – between what Tom hopes to achieve for his day, his life and his career – creates more and more humor.

When a Contrast of Personal Expectations springs from a misunderstanding, it is called a Comedy of Errors. One character believes something that is not true about another character or situation, which results in confusion for other characters. This misunderstanding creates mounting chaos that continues to build humor throughout the story. This Comedy of Errors could be the main plot itself, a subplot involving a few minor characters, or both.

The TV series, *Three's Company,* used this device for nearly every episode. One character heard or saw something another character was doing, and jumped to the wrong conclusion. They then told another character, spreading the misinformation further. As these misinformed characters took action to resolve the imagined problem, their actions were often seen and misinterpreted by yet another character, who then tried to resolve the new imagined problem. The humor in a Comedy of Errors results from mistakes piled on top of mistakes, until a normal everyday situation gets twisted into a complicated melodramatic mess.

MOVIE EXAMPLE: WHILE YOU WERE SLEEPING

Watch the scene from *While You Were Sleeping* when Lucy takes the unconscious Peter to the hospital after rescuing him from being hit by an elevated train. She has such a crush on Peter, whom she has never met, that she mutters she was going to marry him. Watch from the moment the nurse overhears Lucy saying this, to the point when Lucy is told she might have saved the entire family. Then return here.

SUMMARY: WHILE YOU WERE SLEEPING

Lucy rushes into the hospital lobby alongside Peter, who is unconscious on a gurney. She rescued him after thieves attacked him and left him on the elevated train tracks. Though she's never spoken to Peter, her longstanding crush on him leads her to stay and make sure he's all right, but she is kept out of the ER since she's not a family member. Watching the doctors wheel Peter away, she mutters, "I was going to marry him."

A nurse overhears this and is touched. Soon, the nurse leads Lucy into Peter's hospital room, and tells Lucy to let Peter hear her voice. The doctor enters to check on Peter as a loud commotion starts from the hospital corridor. Peter's family swarms in, loud and anxious as they hurry to see Peter. Lucy steps away as the doctor tells the family that Peter is in a coma. The mother is upset because it's Christmas day, and the father asks what happened. Lucy starts to explain, and everyone turns to ask who she is.

The nurse happily explains that Lucy is Peter's fiancée. Lucy is too stunned to speak, as the father begins arguing with the rest of the family over how Peter could be so busy he forgot to tell his family he's engaged. The grandmother sits down suddenly, and the doctor asks Saul, Peter's godfather, if she's all right. Saul tells the doctor she has had several heart attacks recently. She pipes up and says they weren't attacks, but "episodes". Saul tells the doctor there's nothing wrong with her hearing.

A police officer further explains that Lucy jumped onto the tracks to pull Peter away from an oncoming train, saving his life. The family is stunned, as an orderly enters and asks why Lucy is there when only family members are allowed. The father pushes him aside, insisting that Lucy is family, while the doctor tells the orderly that she's Peter's fiancée.

Lucy tries to correct the misunderstanding but the mother comes straight over to her, apologizing for not knowing about her

160

because they've all been so busy. She gushes that she always wanted Peter to find a nice girl, and she's so glad he found Lucy. She gives Lucy a strong hug as she bawls on her shoulder.

Soon afterward, Lucy privately asks the nurse why she told the family that she's Peter's fiancée, when she doesn't even know him. The nurse explains she heard Lucy say she's going to marry him. Lucy angrily tells her she was only talking to herself. The nurse tells her next time she talks to herself, to remind herself she's single and end the conversation.

Lucy asks the nurse what to do, after the mother held her so tight. The nurse doesn't know. Saul walks up to them in the corridor and discusses the grandmother's medications and many medical problems. He then tells Lucy she might have saved the grandmother's life. In fact, she probably saved the whole family, after the shock of finding Peter in a coma. Lucy is speechless, realizing she is now trapped in a phony engagement.

I Think You Misunderstood Me ...

In a Comedy of Errors, a bad situation keeps getting worse. More Errors and confusion pile on top of the original Error, like a snowball rolling down a hill. However, the original Error is usually something small and simple. So something must maintain this Error and give it longevity. It could be that several witnesses jump to the wrong conclusion about a person or situation, so the Error is instantly widespread as they tell others about it.

In the scene from *While You Were Sleeping*, the Error can easily be corrected. But the family is so emotional and aggressive, and Lucy is so shy and accommodating, she simply doesn't fix the problem. She's still reeling from the Error itself.

When she goes to the nurse, we know that shy Lucy can get help to speak up. But then Lucy learns that Peter's grandmother has a weak heart, and the wonderful news of the "engagement" probably helped her survive the shock of finding Peter in a coma. Lucy's unintentional lie has become such a blessing for the entire family that she is now trapped. She *can't* correct the Error. Which means she can't stop the comedy.

Now watch how the initial Error keeps building, growing farther and farther out of control.

MOVIE EXAMPLE: WHILE YOU WERE SLEEPING

Watch the scene from *While You Were Sleeping* when Peter wakes up from his coma to the sound of singing from the hospital staff. By this point, Lucy has started to fall in love with Peter's brother, Jack, making matters even worse. Also, Jack has recently gotten misinformation that Lucy is pregnant, a rumor which made their shaky relationship even less stable. Watch until Peter starts reciting his A B C's. Then return here.

162

SUMMARY: WHILE YOU WERE SLEEPING

On New Year's Day, hospital staff begin singing together, as Peter wakes up from his coma.

We then see Lucy hurrying to meet Peter's father by the hospital elevators, responding to his urgent summons. The father tells her that Peter is awake. She wants to flee but doesn't know how. The father tells her Peter will sure be glad to see her. Lucy just smiles nervously.

Soon, the entire family is gathered around Peter's hospital bed as the doctor wakes Peter up. Lucy glances toward the Exit sign, wondering how to escape. Peter opens his eyes and slowly looks at each family member. After he sees Lucy, he glances back at her and asks who she is. Lucy keeps smiling, not knowing what to say. Saul, the only one who shares her secret, puts his hand to his forehead.

Seeing this, the father is horrified. He exclaims, "He's got amnesia!"

Peter falls unconscious again.

The doctor is soon explaining to the family how selective amnesia works. Lucy tries again to explain that she was never engaged to Peter, but the grandmother cuts her off. Assuming Lucy meant to tell them she was never pregnant, she assures her that Jack already cleared that up.

Jack enters to see Peter. Lucy watches him, wishing she could somehow escape her situation and be with Jack. She pulls Saul into the corridor to ask for help. Saul promises to tell the family about the phony engagement, because they'll accept it better coming from him. But as the doctor leads the family back to Peter's room, Saul ducks down another hallway.

Entering Peter's room, Lucy finds that Saul has disappeared. Peter's parents smile at Lucy, telling Peter he'll want to see her. Peter asks who she is. They tell him to look closely at her, reminding Peter they're engaged, but he doesn't remember it because he has amnesia. Peter worries as an orderly brings him some Jell-O, and asks if he likes Jell-O.

The doctor leads the family out to let Peter rest. Saul peers through a window, making sure it's safe before rejoining the family. Lucy scolds him for disappearing, while Saul insists he only went to the bathroom and assures her he'll tell the family the truth. "When? On my twenty-fifth wedding anniversary?" she says, stalking off with him.

Meanwhile, Peter lies in his hospital bed, thinking. He starts reciting his ABC's to make sure he remembers them.

Make It Stop!!!

In a Comedy of Errors, the Contrast of Personal Expectations continues to grow farther out of control, to the frustration of the main character or characters. As with any story, complications continue to pile up, preventing the main character from reaching their desired goal. Until someone must finally do something extreme to resolve the situation. In the case of *While You Were Sleeping*, Lucy must ultimately confess the truth, though it means losing the new "family" she desperately wants to keep.

However, a Comedy of Errors can occur without involving other characters. It can happen with one single character, whose Personal Expectations are gradually shattered by the circumstances they encounter, based on their personal misunderstanding of events.

TELEVISION EXAMPLE: FRASIER, SEASON 6: "A VALENTINE FOR NILES"

Watch this scene from Season 6 of the television series, *Frasier,* in the episode, "3 Valentines". Watch the 1st story, "A Valentine for Niles", in which Niles Crane prepares for a date while borrowing Frasier's apartment. Note how Niles' Personal Expectations, beliefs and ignorance regarding his situation cause problems that continue to escalate. Watch the entire scene, then return here.

SUMMARY: FRASIER, SEASON 6: "A VALENTINE FOR NILES"

Niles Crane is in the apartment of his brother, Frasier, explaining on the phone that he is borrowing his brother's apartment for a dinner date with a wine connoisseur who has very high standards. Being a fussbudget himself, Niles wants the evening to be perfect. After finishing his call, he soon notices an annoying crease in his trousers that he decides he must iron.

While the apartment's dog, Eddie, watches him, Niles brings an ironing board to the front room to fix the crease. He then notices a loose string on his clothes that he must cut, so sets down the iron to fetch some scissors. He starts running, but then slows to a walk, holding the scissors carefully to avoid an accident. But he still cuts his finger and faints at the sight of his own blood. Eddie licks his face to wake him. Seeing that he spilled some blood on the couch, Niles holds his finger up to avoid looking at it while he gets some rubbing alcohol. After cleaning the couch and fainting once more, he finds a bandage for his finger.

While in the kitchen, he notices an odd burning smell and checks the pots of food he has prepared. Nothing smells off, so he wanders back out to the living room, where he sees smoke rising from the iron that he left on top of his trousers. A fire starts and Niles hurries to put it out, but accidentally tosses the hot trousers onto the couch. The alchohol on the cushions makes the couch burst into flames, and Niles stares in amazement at his predicament. He recovers his senses and grabs a fire extinguisher. When he sprays the foam, he can't control the surging force and ends up spraying all over the center of the apartment, including Eddie, leaving only a few weak squirts to use on the rising flame.

With no choice left, he grabs the pot of soup and tosses it onto the fire, putting it out and leaving the apartment a smoking mess. He then opens the front door and tries to wave out the

166

fumes, but accidentally looks at his uncovered finger once more and faints, lying spread eagle at the entryway in his shorts.

Writing Ideas: The Entire Apartment Was Against Me!

As we see from Niles' escalating misfortunes, a Comedy of Errors does not need to involve other people. When a single character misunderstands some critical information, which is clear to the reader, the humor springs from the character's ignorance of the mounting danger. Niles' fussy nature and the high standards of his unseen dinner date set up the Contrast of Personal Expectations: Niles wants everything to be perfect. This unrealistic Expectation doesn't allow for the mishaps that might occur. So as he tries to perfect his own clothes, he ends up creating further problems for himself, until the entire evening is ruined. Niles' perfect date turns into a fiasco, and we laugh more and more as it gets farther out of his tight-fisted control.

You can create the same scenario by setting up a character's Personal Expectations for something to be perfect: a perfect date, perfect job, perfect family, perfect vacation. Then have things go wrong, creating the worst possible scenarios to spoil their "perfect" Personal Expectations. Start small and let the problem escalate farther out of control.

For example, John, a very conservative businessman starts his first day at a new job, dressed to impress and ready to demonstrate his efficiency and professionalism. Only to discover the boss who hired him has left, and his new boss is a free-spirited "hippie" who lets everyone wear what they want and come and go at odd hours. This, of course, seems like utter chaos to John.

Or let's say Julianna's boyfriend, Chuck, tells her he has something important to discuss with her that night. Julianna expects Chuck to propose, but she doesn't want him to know she suspects. Perhaps Chuck really *does* plan to propose, and we can see the situation from his perspective as well as Julianna's. The Expectation is for a perfect romantic evening, culminating in the promise of a lifetime love.

But Chuck's restaurant reservations cannot be confirmed and his car's battery quits. So they must walk, in her satin dress and expensive heels, several blocks to find a greasy spoon restaurant, where they encounter unsavory servers and customers. Its only bathroom reeks, the power goes out, their food is raw or burnt, and they keep getting interrupted whenever Julianna prompts Chuck to tell her what he meant to discuss with her.

Later, they hike back to find Chuck's car is no longer parked in the tow-away zone where he left it, as Chuck realizes he left the engagement ring in the glove compartment. They use his last few dollars to hire a cab to take him most of the way home, then walk the rest of the way, tired and filthy. When Julianna prompts him again to tell her what he wanted to discuss, he sheepishly tells her he forgot. So much for the perfect romantic evening.

Try this out yourself. Set up the perfect Expectation, then list out all the things that could ruin that Expectation. Make most or all of those problems happen in your story, and you'll have something funny to share!

And Now, Back to You …

So What Do I Do With This?

Ready to practice? Now that we have discussed the various forms of humorous contrast, you're more than ready to start adding humor to your writing. Remember, it doesn't have to be hysterical. It just needs to be amusing enough to make your reader enjoy your characters and scenarios more and keep reading. The purpose is to add entertainment and affection for your story, even if it's just a smile on your reader's lips.

So don't pressure yourself to be as funny as the stand-up comic you watched last night. It probably won't happen. But you can add enough humor to make readers fall in love with your characters and your story, and you'll get better with practice.

Here's your assignment.

Write a funny story, 5-15 pages long, double-spaced, about a person who is forced to deal with someone or something that is the exact opposite of what they want. This can fall into any of the four types of humorous contrast we discussed:

1) Opposite personality (Contrast of People – Clowns & Straight Men)

2) Opposite environment (Contrast of Normal or Abnormal World)

3) Opposite perception (Contrast of Perspectives)

4) Opposite result (Contrast of Personal Expectations that someone hopes for, which could also be Comedy of Errors if it's based on a misunderstanding)

When you're done, have a few trustworthy friends read it and tell you if it worked. That is, did it make the story more enjoyable? Did it even make it genuinely cute and funny in places?

171

For further help, you can contact me to request a paid critique. I focus on the positive of what you're doing well (and so should you), along with providing suggestions for improvement. You can contact me with your request or for any other feedback at Randall@RandallAllenDunn.com.

Sooo … Good-bye!

I hope this has proven helpful. Feel free to contact me with questions or feedback.

Randall Allen Dunn

RandallAllenDunn.com

Randall@RandallAllenDunn.com

Now go be hilarious!

(:^D

Meanwhile, please enjoy this funny excerpt from my action-adventure thriller,

HIGH ADVENTURE:

THE SOLOMON RING OF KILIMANJARO

CHAPTER ONE
OUT ON A LIMB

"Jack! *Jaaaack !*"

Jack Benjamin squinted through the brown clump of hair hanging over his right eye. Below him, Amanda's long, ruffled skirt swirled around her heels, dangling over the excited lion thirty feet below. Jack gritted his teeth as she hung from his bruised right arm, wishing she weighed sixty pounds less.

"Still – here. Hang on, Love."

"It's pacing!" she cried, following the animal's movement. Her straw-blond hair spun about her neck like a panicked toy top. "It's licking its *lips!*"

"Lions – do that." He hated to waste energy by answering back. But he couldn't ignore her rising British lilt.

The thorny gray branch creaked under their combined weight as Jack's left hand strained to reach Amanda's wrist. His 200 pounds and her "just-a-hair-over-a-hundred" – which felt more like 120 to Jack – were too much to ask of the old acacia tree.

Amanda's hand trembled in his. "I shall say it again: coming to Africa was a *bad idea!*"

"Noted." Jack ground his teeth and firmed up his hold. Thorns cut into the thighs of his tan trousers. "I need your arm. Can you – help?"

174

"Yes, of course. How?" Her golden hair flipped back from pleading eyes as she worked to close the skirt around her legs. "How am I to help? *Help* me to *help!*"

"Find something to hoist yourself up. And never mind your modesty. He wants to eat you, not *court* you."

She fidgeted in his grip. "You've no idea how difficult it is to wear dresses here, tripping over folds of fabric every time you run somewhere – ."

"Right. I don't know!" He leaned further out and firmed up his grip on her slender wrist as the mess of hair fell over his eyes again. The lion seemed to notice his struggle and stopped its pacing.

"Don't yell at me!"

"Don't wiggle about."

"You're not the one being *eaten!*"

"No one's being eaten. Just –." A low, creaking moan rose from the base of the limb. They fell silent, awaiting further warnings. A tiny snap of the wood sent a fresh trickle of sweat sliding down Jack's cheek. It clung to the bottom of his square jaw, while the lion continued to watch and wait. "I need – your hand."

He had to make her relax in his grip and build back his strength. Revealing his fatigue would only panic her more. Scores of unseen guinea fowl hooted from the surrounding trees, their kak-kak-kak-kak's sounding like a slow-starting motorcar. *Think, Jack, think!*

If he was seated in his Avro 504 biplane, he would know exactly what to do and how to do it. If Amanda was dangling alongside his cockpit, he could roll the plane in the opposite direction with one hand, letting gravity drop her into his lap. Or he could pitch forward slightly to help her climb onto the wing and up into the front seat. But here in the dense African bush, he could only grit his teeth.

Amanda's free hand stretched toward his. *Thank the Lord she had settled some!* Straddling the branch tightly with his thighs, Jack leaned forward. Amanda's doe-like eyes searched his

175

with renewed hope as he reached for her delicate, grasping fingers.

The branch cracked like a gunshot.

Amanda's shriek scattered a flock of guinea fowl from nearby trees as the limb bent. Jack swallowed a chunk of air as they slid a few inches down. He hugged the trembling branch as it scraped into his chest. The shifting settled and Jack listened for further signs of cracking over Amanda's panic and the lion's impatient growls. "Quiet, Love, it's all right."

"You're squeezing too tight! Let *go!*"

"Sorry. Can't let go just yet, of course ..."

Her eyes blazed up at him like fiery blue diamonds. "I'm *quite* sure you know what I meant!"

Jack flexed his thighs to lock his legs on the rough bark as the thorns dug in deeper. Relieved of some pressure, he curled his left arm further around the branch and seized Amanda's wrist, securing her with both hands. He sighed deeply as life returned to his right arm.

"Jack," Amanda called, almost giddy. "I've found a spotty gray vine."

Jack's stomach went hollow. He raised his head and all became clear.

The arching snake fixed a cold stare on him from three feet away. It lifted its chin imperiously, as if offended by the disturbance in its temporary tree home. Jack had seen poisonous puff adders like this one in swamps and on the grass roofs of huts here in Niura. It was a young male, distinguished by the peacock's eye design on its silvery skin. Simply put, it was "gray and spotty".

A gentle breeze tickled Jack's neck, reminding him to breathe. He did so in a slow, even rhythm, quieting every nerve as the serpent's black eyes bulged and waited for him to explain his business there. Amanda swung merrily from his locked arms, as he prepared to transfer her "hair-over-a-hundred" pounds back to the aching right hand.

Jack prayed for the Lord to help him switch hands without tensing his neck too much. And to do it fast enough to deal with the snake before any fresh sweat rolled off his forehead. If a salty

176

drop trickled out from behind Jack's matted clump of hair, the adder would surely take a lick.

"Almost – got it." Amanda sounded like a child playing on a swingset.

Jack's anguished thighs gripped the branch tighter. Amanda wouldn't be so proud when she yanked the adder's tail and it sank its fangs into his nose. Or when they all fell to the hard ground, effectively setting the lion's dinner table.

Jack relaxed his face and neck as he tensed his right arm. His biceps flared in protest as he smoothly shifted Amanda's weight over to free his left hand.

If he had flinched, the snake ignored it. Locking Jack in its icy gaze, it took no notice as Jack's free hand drew quietly up alongside the branch. No notice as it slid slowly, gingerly toward Jack's hip.

"Almost – al-*most!*" Amanda sang beneath him. Her swinging weight produced a definite film of sweat on Jack's forehead. It would stream into the snake's view any second.

With two barely audible pops, Jack unsnapped the sheath strapped to his leg. Beneath the serpent's bottomless eyes, its throat bulged in and out like a bullfrog's. Jack slid the 16" curved panga from its compartment as if he had all the time in the world.

"GOT IT!" Amanda cried.

The snake darted for Jack's eyes quicker than Jack could think. Jack had already rolled the machete about in his fist to hack at the adder's lunging neck. His single strike chopped through the skin and between the vertebrae. Amanda's shifting weight tugged Jack to the right and the adder's severed head sailed past him, its venomous jaws locked open.

"Jack. Jack, it's not a vine. It's a – it's a –!" Amanda's skirt spun in a frenzy as she gripped the adder's tail, its other end spiraling above the lion's head and scattering its blood like a water hose.

"I know. It was –."

"It's a *HEADLESS SNAKE!*" she screamed, dropping the spineless, bleeding carcass. "Ew, ew, *EWW!*"

Jack's shoulder wrenched as Amanda spun about in horror. The hopeful lion padded over to the snake, but quickly dismissed it and returned its gaze to the frantic legs dangling overhead.

"Where would a creature like that *come* from?" Amanda yammered. "What kind of jungle *IS* this?"

"Just hang on."

"Haven't I been? Eep!"

The groaning limb pitched them another few inches, like a grandfather weary of the rambunctious children playing on his lap. They hung there, gasping as the lion's grunts followed after them.

Jack struggled for her wrist again but couldn't stretch far enough. "Amanda, take my hand."

"I *have* your hand! Or the lion would be *eating!*"

"Your *other* hand!"

She stretched toward him. "I can't reach!" she cried, her voice rising in panic. She twisted about wildly, her dress attracting the lion like a bullfighter's cloak.

"Try! Stretch!"

"I *am!*" she gasped, her cheeks reddening. Hanging by one arm had also taken its toll on her. She couldn't raise her other arm enough to meet Jack's grasping fingers. She clawed the air frantically as the anxious lion sat higher.

Still too far.

"Try again," Jack urged in his gentlest tone. "A bit farther."

She strained toward him, licking her lips to concentrate as the lion licked his. Jack and Amanda's fingertips still missed each other by half an inch.

Her struggles dwindled. "I'm to be eaten by a lion."

"No, you aren't! Come on, a bit more!"

"Two years of our lives here, wasted."

"Nonsense! Just settle down, and –."

"We've never settled down," she sniffled. "No home. No children. Perhaps if I had –."

Jack squeezed tighter as her grip loosened. "Amanda! Don't let go! Trust me, I'll pull you up. Reach once more." His arm begged for a release that his mind refused to give it. If she could only stretch a little further. Just *half an inch!*

The lion stared like a marble statue, as if sensing that Jack's strength was nearly spent. They teetered forward on the branch again and Jack's hand almost drew back to cover his left pocket. The protective reflex reminded him of his original plan for that afternoon. "Amanda, *wait!* I've something *for* you."

She didn't turn to see what he dug from his rear pocket. He might as well have presented it to the attentive lion.

"Amanda, look. This is for *you*, Love, *take* it!"

She turned toward him, confused by the little diamond ring pressed between his thumb and forefinger. Then she frowned. "Must we do this now?"

He smiled as if the cracking bark wasn't chewing away his legs. As if her dangling weight did not feel like that of a pregnant elephant. "Amanda Ruth Regent – Will you marry me?"

Frantic tears curved around her large cheeks. "Do you intend to drop me if I say 'no'?"

You're set on killing us both, aren't you, Love? Jack thought, as he maintained his agonized smile. *"Take – the ring."*

Her grip tightened again on his numbing fist. "Don't think I don't know what you're up to," she said, straining toward him. "Having me reach for your hand – while I accept your ring – Killing two birds – with one stone. – So to speak."

Her fingers brushed the diamond's edge.

Sweat dripped through the curved ends of Jack's hair as he stretched his arm. The droplets fell past Amanda to disappear halfway down to the lion. "Just hold onto it for a bit. – while you consider it."

She screwed up her face as she clawed the air. "I *have* considered it. – Must you make everything – so difficult?"

Letting herself swing freely, Amanda used her momentum to help stretch as the lion studied her repeated attempts.

Jack felt as though his throbbing pulse might burst through his neck and forearm. The jungle fell silent, as if Amanda's struggle had enthralled every living creature. "Come on, don't let me drop this."

179

Amanda bared her teeth, snarling like an enraged poodle. Her wrath might have been directed at Jack, his ring, the continent of Africa, or the shortness of her own arm. If she fell at that moment, she and the lion might have been evenly matched.

"A bit further," he urged. "Almost. Almost – *Yes!*"

Her slim fingers found and clutched the ring's protruding diamond. Jack pulled her up and rolled his meaty palm around her fingers for a better grip. She rose toward him by inches while Jack's entire torso shook. Until she grabbed hold of the thorny limb and Jack adjusted his grip to take her by her elbows, then by her upper arms, then reaching her slim waist as she leaned her neck against his and rested with him in the tree.

Amanda released an exhausted sigh and observed the disappointed lion from their safe perch. She stroked Jack's cheek with a grateful smile. "Well, aren't you clever?"

He caressed her hand and smiled back into her hypnotic eyes with immense relief.

The branch snapped.

ADVENTURE TAKES FLIGHT

Missionary flier Jack Benjamin braves crocodile-infested streams, savage warriors, and diabolical deathtraps to rescue his danger-prone fiancée, Amanda, from Imperial German forces. With his modified Avro 504 biplane and his Maasai warrior friend, Mayani, he races to protect the mysterious Solomon Ring, hidden within a secret chamber of Mount Kilimanjaro and rumored to bestow King Solomon's wisdom on anyone who wears it. Can he arrive in time to save Amanda and stop the Germans from using the Solomon Ring to conquer all of Africa?

181

Come Along for the Ride.

Disfigured in childhood by a bizarre talking wolf, teenage Helena Basque discovers an army of such wolves threatening her French village. When no one else takes action, Helena dons the red hood and cloak she was forbidden to wear as a child, then arms herself with a repeating crossbow to wage a private war against the monsters, refusing to stop or slow down until she destroys every last one of them. Whatever it costs.

She was grateful to get into Gameland.

Now she's desperate to get back out.

Amy Raven insists she's innocent. She never saw the steroids until her coach found them in Amy's locker. Expelled and friendless, she takes a dead end job at Grater Gameland, an abandoned theme park that's preparing to make a comeback.

But Gunther Grater's not interested in re-opening his father's park. He only wants to use it to trap Amy for himself. And he's enlisted nine other gamers to compete in a deadly hunt to track her down.

Given a pair of night vision goggles and a hunting knife, Amy finds herself fighting an onslaught of predators, each with their own deranged plans for her. To survive, she must outwit, outmaneuver, and outrun each one of them. But how can she escape when even the rides are rigged against her?

The only way out is through.

Coming in 2017 ...

Hooves thundering through the forest.

Cloak billowing in the wind.

Repeating crossbow armed and ready.

Red Rider REVOLUTION

She's only getting started.

KEEP UP WITH HELENA & OTHER HEROES.
Subscribe to the Packing Action Newsletter Datafile
at www.RandallAllenDunn.com.